Anonymous

Philanthropy and Social Progress

Anonymous

Philanthropy and Social Progress

ISBN/EAN: 9783337407612

Printed in Europe, USA, Canada, Australia, Japan

Cover: Foto ©Suzi / pixelio.de

More available books at **www.hansebooks.com**

Social Progress

SEVEN ESSAYS

BY

MISS JANE ADDAMS, ROBERT A. WOODS
FATHER J. O. S. HUNTINGTON
PROFESSOR FRANKLIN H. GIDDINGS
AND BERNARD BOSANQUET

DELIVERED BEFORE

The School of Applied Ethics

AT PLYMOUTH, MASS.

DURING THE SESSION OF 1892

WITH INTRODUCTION
By PROFESSOR HENRY C. ADAMS

CONTENTS.

PAGE

INTRODUCTION. By Professor Henry C. Adams . v

I. THE SUBJECTIVE NECESSITY FOR SOCIAL
SETTLEMENTS. By Miss Jane Addams . 1

II. THE OBJECTIVE VALUE OF A SOCIAL SET-
TLEMENT. By Miss Jane Addams . . 27

III. THE UNIVERSITY SETTLEMENT IDEA. By
Robert A. Woods 57

IV. PHILANTHROPY—ITS SUCCESS AND FAIL-
URE. By Father James O. S. Huntington . 98

V. PHILANTHROPY AND MORALITY.
By Father James O. S. Huntington . . 157

VI. THE ETHICS OF SOCIAL PROGRESS. By
Professor Franklin H. Giddings . . . 208

VII. THE PRINCIPLES AND CHIEF DANGERS OF
THE ADMINISTRATION OF CHARITY. By
Bernard Bosanquet, M.A.. LL.D.. . . . 249

INTRODUCTION.

By HENRY C. ADAMS, Ph.D.,

Professor of Political Economy and Finance in the University
of Michigan.

THE lectures brought together in this volume
were first delivered before the School of Applied
Ethics at its summer session, 1892. The subject
treated is sufficiently important, and the lectures
themselves of sufficient interest, to claim the attention of the public without explanation or introduction; but they will lose nothing in the interest
which they have for the reader, and they may
possibly be the better understood, should a statement be made of the place they occupied in the
general instruction of the school. In order to do
this a word must be said respecting the school
itself.

There is nothing new in the assertion that the
complex relations of modern life cannot be satis-
factorily adjusted except the claims of man's moral
nature be frankly and fully recognized; but this
thought has, we believe, been made the central
idea in a systematic and somewhat comprehensive
curriculum of study for the first time by those

who organized the School of Applied Ethics. There are three departments in this school. The first of these is the department of Comparative Religion, in which the leading principles of the great religions of the world, and the effect of these principles on the lives of the people who believe them, are made the subject of special investigation.

The Science of Ethics constitutes the second department of instruction. In this department search is made for the fundamental basis of moral conduct by a comparative study of the ethical systems that have characterized the various civilizations, and given color to different epochs of history. Here, also, the problem of providing adequate moral instruction for the children of our common schools, is recognized as one of the most important pedagogical problems of our day.

The third department of instruction is that of Economics. It was in this department that the lectures collected in the present volume were first delivered. Instruction in Economics, in a School of Applied Ethics, is doubtless recognition of the fact, that, inasmuch as the most significant changes of the nineteenth century are industrial in character, the most pressing of the practical questions of right and wrong find their root in industrial relationships. It is not enough to urge right conduct or high motives upon those who control the business affairs of the day in order to infuse morality into business conduct; for there is no hope of

making moral conduct general until such legal
and social conditions are created, that he who follows a high ideal of justice in business dealings,
can hope for a fair degree of business success. It
is, therefore, essential for the economist who believes that moral sentiments should be brought to
bear on industrial life, to re-examine the fundamental principles of his science, and to analyze
again the social structure through which those
principles assert themselves, in order to discover
what form of business organization, or what expression of industrial rights, will call into natural
and spontaneous exercise the tremendous force of
moral character which, since the time of the old
guilds and the canon law, has lain almost dormant
in industrial life. It was this idea which induced
those who organized the School of Applied Ethics
to recognize Economics as worthy a place in a curriculum of study which has for its aim a revival of
confidence in the moral dignity of man.

In the session of 1892, all the studies in the
department of Economics centred about the idea
of social progress. The lectures of the first week
traced the Changes in Economic Theory since the
Time of John Stuart Mill. It was their purpose to
leave the impression that the economist is gradually
changing his point of view, and that political economy, while ceasing to be an industrial philosophy
of a class, is coming to be a comprehensive philosophy of industrial society. The second week's

instruction was devoted to the Theory of Social
Progress, being a study in sociology.   One lecture
of this course finds place in the present volume
under the title, " The Ethics of Social Progress."
The instruction of the third week considered ' The
Function of Law in Social Progress,' and was
devoted especially to the consideration of self-help
and legislation for promoting it.   The subject for
the fourth week's instruction was ' Philanthropy
in Social Progress,' and it is the lectures delivered
during this week that have been collected and
are now presented in book form.   The fifth week
gave a ' Statistical Presentation of Industrial
Problems,' and the sixth week was devoted to
' A Critical Study of the Labor and Monopoly
Problem,' it being assumed that these problems
constituted the most serious obstacle which society
encounters in further development.

It certainly adds something to the appreciation
of this volume to learn that its chapters were a
part of an extended investigation bearing on the
problem of social progress; it gives to the subject
a wider horizon, and brings to the discussion the
sympathy of a comprehensive purpose.   And what
is especially attractive is, that all contributors to
this volume, with the exception of Professor Giddings, are practical philanthropists, — that is to
say, they have devoted their lives to the realization of the principles which they advocate, and,
consequently, the views and opinions which they

express come with the force of personal experience.

Miss Jane Addams, who writes the first and the second chapters, is the guiding spirit of Hull House in Chicago, probably the most influential Settlement in this country; and when she speaks of " The Subjective Necessity for Social Settlements," she tells of her own experience and the experience of many cultivated men and women, her co-workers, who find that life has a new meaning the moment they breathe the atmosphere of what she so aptly calls the "*renaissance* of Christianity." And when, turning to the other side of the question, she writes of the " Objective Value of Social Settlements," it is the story of Hull House that claims attention.

The third chapter in this volume is entitled " The Society Settlement Idea," and is contributed by Mr. Robert A. Woods. Mr. Woods is a recent graduate of Amherst College, and finds in his connection with the Andover House of Boston a life which calls forth every faculty of the mind and satisfies every aspiration of healthful activity. Assuming that Social Settlements are destined to increase in number and influence, he draws on personal experience to answer such inquiries as naturally present themselves to those who purpose entering upon such work. The chapter is a most instructive and helpful one.

The fourth and fifth chapters are contributed by

the Rev. James O. S. Huntington, better known, perhaps, as Father Huntington, of the Order of the Holy Cross. In the fourth chapter he discusses "Philanthropy — Its Success and Failure," and in the fifth chapter he treats of "Philanthropy and Morality." These chapters fascinate the reader, because they tell without apology or palliation so many things we know to be true. Who can deny that the same rules of conduct should apply to the rich, as the rich in bestowing their charities assume to apply to the poor? Who does not know that much of our so-called philanthropy tends to blunt the edge of moral perception, and, consequently, to perpetuate those conditions which seem to make philanthropy necessary? Few of us care to express truths so unpalatable, and Father Huntington has rendered a marked service in the strong protest which he here urges against the charities of our day. He shows to the discerning mind that a philanthropy which is satisfied when the cry of the sufferer is hushed has no place among the permanent forces of social progress.

Professor Giddings presents in the sixth chapter of this volume a carefully considered analysis of the "Ethics of Social Progress." In the final chapter Mr. Bernard Bosanquet, himself an active member of the Charity Organization of London, gives the experience of that society, under the title, "The Administration of Charity."

Such a series of lectures ought to arouse wide-spread interest. Their chief characteristic is a strongly marked vein of democratic sentiment. Not, of course, democracy as "a form of government," but as a social ideal, a purpose, a feeling; the democracy of the theorist who asserts for God a common fatherhood, or of the humanist who asserts for man a common brotherhood. Nor can it be said that this feeling is pure sentiment; it is, at the same time, a social necessity. Specialization in modern life has increased the dependencies of men and classes to such a degree that interdependence is a thing which is felt, rather than an idea to be reasoned about. This is the explanation of the unusual interest which the last quarter of a century bestows on social and industrial problems. Society is coming to be in fact organic, and the claim of a perfect organism that all parts should find harmony of life in the recognition of a common aim, shows itself in the attitude which large numbers of persons are assuming before the vexed problems of the day. And I doubt not that many who find this book attractive will do so because it expresses in vigorous and decided language a feeling of which most of us are at least dimly conscious. It is a privilege to introduce such a book to the reading public.

H. C. A.

PHILANTHROPY AND SOCIAL PROGRESS.

—∞⚬⚬—

I.

THE SUBJECTIVE NECESSITY FOR SOCIAL SETTLEMENTS.

By Jane Addams, "Hull House," Chicago.

Hull House, which was Chicago's first Settlement, was established in September, 1889. It represented no association, but was opened by two women, backed by many friends, in the belief that the mere foothold of a house, easily accessible, ample in space, hospitable and tolerant in spirit, situated in the midst of the large foreign colonies which so easily isolate themselves in American cities, would be in itself a serviceable thing for Chicago. Hull House endeavors to make social intercourse express the growing sense of the economic unity of society. It is an effort to add the social function to democracy. It was opened on the theory that the dependence of classes on each other is reciprocal; and that as "the social relation

is essentially a reciprocal relation, it gave a form
of expression that has peculiar value."

This paper is an attempt to treat of the subjective necessity for Social Settlements, to analyze the
motives which underlie a movement based not only
upon conviction, but genuine emotion. Hull House
of Chicago is used as an illustration, but so far as
the analysis is faithful, it obtains wherever educated young people are seeking an outlet for that
sentiment of universal brotherhood which the
best spirit of our times is forcing from an emotion
into a motive.

I have divided the motives which constitute the
subjective pressure toward Social Settlements into
three great lines: the first contains the desire to
make the entire social organism democratic, to extend democracy beyond its political expression;
the second is the impulse to share the race life,
and to bring as much as possible of social energy
and the accumulation of civilization to those portions of the race which have little ; the third springs
from a certain *renaissance* of Christianity, a movement toward its early humanitarian aspects.

It is not difficult to see that although America
is pledged to the democratic ideal, the view of
democracy has been partial, and that its best
achievement thus far has been pushed along the
line of the franchise. Democracy has made little
attempt to assert itself in social affairs. We have
refused to move beyond the position of its eigh-

teenth-century leaders, who believed that political
equality alone would secure all good to all men.
We conscientiously followed the gift of the ballot
hard upon the gift of freedom to the negro, but we
are quite unmoved by the fact that he lives among
us in a practical social ostracism. We hasten to
give the franchise to the immigrant from a sense
of justice, from a tradition that he ought to have
it, while we dub him with epithets deriding his
past life or present occupation, and feel no duty to
invite him to our houses. We are forced to acknowledge that it is only in our local and national
politics that we try very hard for the ideal so dear
to those who were enthusiasts when the century
was young. We have almost given it up as our
ideal in social intercourse. There are city wards
in which many of the votes are sold for drinks
and dollars; still there is a remote pretence, at
least a fiction current, that a man's vote is his
own. The judgment of the voter is consulted and
an opportunity for remedy given. There is not
even a theory in the social order, not a shadow
answering to the polls in politics. The time may
come when the politician who sells one by one to
the highest bidder all the offices in his grasp, will
not be considered more base in his code of morals,
more hardened in his practice, than the woman
who constantly invites to her receptions those
alone who bring her an equal social return, who
shares her beautiful surroundings only with those

who minister to a liking she has for successful
social events. In doing this is she not just as
unmindful of the common weal, as unscrupulous
in her use of power, as is any city " boss " who con-
sults only the interests of the "ring"?

In politics "bossism" arouses a scandal. It goes
on in society constantly and is only beginning to
be challenged.   Our consciences are becoming
tender in regard to the lack of democracy in social
affairs.   We are perhaps entering upon the second
phase of democracy, as the French philosophers
entered upon the first, somewhat bewildered by its
logical conclusions.   The social organism has
broken down through large districts of our great
cities.   Many of the people living there are very
poor, the majority of them without leisure or
energy for anything but the gain of subsistence.
They move often from one wretched lodging to
another.   They live for the moment side by side,
many of them without knowledge of each other,
without fellowship, without local tradition or
public spirit, without social organization of any
kind.   Practically nothing is done to remedy this.
The people who might do it, who have the social
tact and training, the large houses, and the traditions and custom of hospitality, live in other parts
of the city.   The club-houses, libraries, galleries,
and semi-public conveniences for social life are also
blocks away.   We find working-men organized into
armies of producers because men of executive abil-

ity and business sagacity have found it to their interests thus to organize them. But these working-men are not organized socially; although living in crowded tenement-houses, they are living without a corresponding social contact. The chaos is as great as it would be were they working in huge factories without foreman or superintendent. Their ideas and resources are cramped. The desire for higher social pleasure is extinct. They have no share in the traditions and social energy which make for progress. Too often their only place of meeting is a saloon, their only host a bartender; a local demagogue forms their public opinion. Men of ability and refinement, of social power and university cultivation, stay away from them. Personally, I believe the men who lose most are those who thus stay away. But the paradox is here: when cultivated people do stay away from a certain portion of the population, when all social advantages are persistently withheld, it may be for years, the result itself is pointed at as a reason, is used as an argument, for the continued withholding.

It is constantly said that because the masses have never had social advantages they do not want them, that they are heavy and dull, and that it will take political or philanthropic machinery to change them. This divides a city into rich and poor; into the favored, who express their sense of the social obligation by gifts of money, and into the unfavored, who express it by clamoring for a

"share" — both of them actuated by a vague sense
of justice. This division of the city would be
more justifiable, however, if the people who thus
isolate themselves on certain streets and use
their social ability for each other gained enough
thereby and added sufficient to the sum total of
social progress to justify the withholding of the
pleasures and results of that progress from so many
people who ought to have them. But they cannot accomplish this. "The social spirit discharges
itself in many forms, and no one form is adequate
to its total expression." We are all uncomfortable
in regard to the sincerity of our best phrases,
because we hesitate to translate our philosophy
into the deed.

It is inevitable that those who feel most keenly
this insincerity and partial living should be our
young people, our so-called educated young people
who accomplish little toward the solution of this
social problem, and who bear the brunt of being
cultivated into unnourished, over-sensitive lives.
They have been shut off from the common labor
by which they live and which is a great source of
moral and physical health. They feel a fatal want
of harmony between their theory and their lives, a
lack of co-ordination between thought and action.
I think it is hard for us to realize how seriously
many of them are taking to the notion of human
brotherhood, how eagerly they long to give tangi-
ble expression to the democratic ideal. These

young men and women, longing to socialize their democracy, are animated by certain hopes.

These hopes may be loosely formulated thus: that if in a democratic country nothing can be permanently achieved save through the masses of the people, it will be impossible to establish a higher political life than the people themselves crave; that it is difficult to see how the notion of a higher civic life can be fostered save through common intercourse; that the blessings which we associate with a life of refinement and cultivation can be made universal and must be made universal if they are to be permanent; that the good we secure for ourselves is precarious and uncertain, is floating in mid-air, until it is secured for all of us and incorporated into our common life.

These hopes are responsible for results in various directions, pre-eminently in the extension of educational advantages. We find that all educational matters are more democratic in their political than in their social aspects. The public schools in the poorest and most crowded wards of the city are inadequate to the number of children, and many of the teachers are ill-prepared and overworked; but in each ward there is an effort to secure public education. The school-house itself stands as a pledge that the city recognizes and endeavors to fulfil the duty of educating its children. But what becomes of these children

when they are no longer in public schools? Many
of them never come under the influence of a professional teacher nor a cultivated friend after they
are twelve. Society at large does little for their
intellectual development. The dream of transcen-
dentalists that each New England village would
be a university, that every child taken from the
common school would be put into definite lines of
study and mental development, had its unfulfilled
beginning in the village lyceum and lecture courses,
and has its feeble representative now in the multitude of clubs for study which are so sadly restricted
to educators, to the leisure class, or only to the
advanced and progressive wage-workers.

The University Extension movement — certainly
when it is closely identified with Settlements —
would not confine learning to those who already
want it, or to those who, by making an effort, can
gain it, or to those among whom professional educators are already at work, but would take it to the
tailors of East London and the dock-laborers of the
Thames. It requires tact and training, love of
learning, and the conviction of the justice of its
diffusion to give it to people whose intellectual
faculties are untrained and disused. But men in
England are found who do it successfully, and it is
believed there are men and women in America who
can do it. I also believe that the best work in
University Extension can be done in Settlements,
where the teaching will be further socialized, where

the teacher will grapple his students, not only by formal lectures, but by every hook possible to the fuller intellectual life which he represents. This teaching requires distinct methods, for it is true of people who have been allowed to remain undeveloped and whose faculties are inert and sterile, that they cannot take their learning heavily. It has to be diffused in a social atmosphere. Information held in solution, a medium of fellowship and goodwill can be assimilated by the dullest.

If education is, as Froebel defined it, "deliverance," deliverance of the forces of the body and mind, then the untrained must first be delivered from all constraint and rigidity before their faculties can be used. Possibly one of the most pitiful periods in the drama of the much-praised young American who attempts to rise in life is the time when his educational requirements seem to have locked him up and made him rigid. He fancies himself shut off from his uneducated family and misunderstood by his friends. He is bowed down by his mental accumulations and often gets no farther than to carry them through life as a great burden. Not once has he had a glimpse of the delights of knowledge. Intellectual life requires for its expansion and manifestation the influence and assimilation of the interests and affections of others. Mazzini, that greatest of all democrats, who broke his heart over the condition of the South European peasantry, said: "Education is

not merely a necessity of true life by which the
individual renews his vital force in the vital force
of humanity; it is a Holy Communion with generations dead and living, by which he fecundates all
his faculties.   When he is withheld from this Communion for generations, as the Italian peasant has
been, we point our finger at him and say, 'He is
like a beast of the field; he must be controlled by
force.' "   Even to this it is sometimes added that
it is absurd to educate him, immoral to disturb his
content.   We stupidly use again the effect as an
argument for a continuance of the cause.   It is
needless to say that a Settlement is a protest
against a restricted view of education, and makes
it possible for every educated man or woman with
a teaching faculty to find out those who are ready
to be taught.   The social and educational activities
of a Settlement are but differing manifestations of
the attempt to socialize democracy, as is the existence of the settlement itself.

I find it somewhat difficult to formulate the second line of motives which I believe to constitute
the trend of the subjective pressure toward the
Settlement.   There is something primordial about
these motives, but I am perhaps over-bold in desig-
nating them as a great desire to share the race life.
We all bear traces of the starvation struggle which
for so long made up the life of the race.   Our very
organism holds memories and glimpses of that long
life of our ancestors which still goes on among so

many of our contemporaries. Nothing so deadens the sympathies and shrivels the power of enjoyment as the persistent keeping away from the great opportunities for helpfulness and a continual ignoring of the starvation struggle which makes up the life of at least half the race. To shut one's self away from that half of the race life is to shut one's self away from the most vital part of it; it is to live out but half the humanity which we have been born heir to and to use but half our faculties. We have all had longings for a fuller life which should include the use of these faculties. These longings are the physical complement of the "Intimations of Immortality" on which no ode has yet been written. To portray these would be the work of a poet, and it is hazardous for any but a poet to attempt it.

You may remember the forlorn feeling which occasionally seizes you when you arrive early in the morning a stranger in a great city. The stream of laboring people goes past you as you gaze through the plate-glass window of your hotel. You see hard-working men lifting great burdens; you hear the driving and jostling of huge carts. Your heart sinks with a sudden sense of futility. The door opens behind you and you turn to the man who brings you in your breakfast with a quick sense of human fellowship. You find yourself praying that you may never lose your hold on it all. A more poetic prayer would be that the

great mother breasts of our common humanity,
with its labor and suffering and its homely comforts, may never be withheld from you. You turn
helplessly to the waiter. You feel that it would
be almost grotesque to claim from him the sympathy you crave. Civilization has placed you far
apart, but you resent your position with a sudden
sense of snobbery. Literature is full of portrayals
of these glimpses. They come to shipwrecked
men on rafts; they overcome the differences of
an incongruous multitude when in the presence
of a great danger or when moved by a common
enthusiasm. They are not, however, confined to
such moments, and if we were in the habit of telling them to each other, the recital would be as
long as the tales of children are, when they sit
down on the green grass and confide to each other
how many times they have remembered that they
lived once before. If these tales are the stirring
of inherited impressions, just so surely is the other
the striving of inherited powers.

"There is nothing after disease, indigence, and
a sense of guilt so fatal to health and to life itself
as the want of a proper outlet for active faculties."
I have seen young girls suffer and grow sensibly
lowered in vitality in the first years after they
leave school. In our attempt then to give a girl
pleasure and freedom from care we succeed, for
the most part, in making her pitifully miserable.
She finds "life" so different from what she ex-

pected it to be. She is besotted with innocent little ambitions, and does not understand this apparent waste of herself, this elaborate preparation, if no work is provided for her. There is a heritage of noble obligation which young people accept and long to perpetuate. The desire for action, the wish to right wrong and alleviate suffering, haunts them daily. Society smiles at it indulgently instead of making it of value to itself. The wrong to them begins even farther back, when we restrain the first childish desires for " doing good " and tell them that they must wait until they are older and better fitted. We intimate that social obligation begins at a fixed date, forgetting that it begins with birth itself. We treat them as children who, with strong-growing limbs, are allowed to use their legs but not their arms, or whose legs are daily carefully exercised that after awhile their arms may be put to high use. We do this in spite of the protest of the best educators, Locke and Pestalozzi. We are fortunate in the mean time if their unused members do not weaken and disappear. They do sometimes. There are a few girls who, by the time they are " educated," forget their old childish desires to help the world and to play with poor little girls " who haven't playthings." Parents are often inconsistent. They deliberately expose their daughters to knowledge of the distress in the world. They send them to hear missionary addresses on famines

in India and China; they accompany them to
lectures on the suffering in Siberia; they agitate
together over the forgotten region of East London.
In addition to this, from babyhood the altruistic
tendencies of these daughters are persistently cultivated. They are taught to be self-forgetting and
self-sacrificing, to consider the good of the Whole
before the good of the Ego. But when all this
information and culture show results, when the
daughter comes back from college and begins to
recognize her social claim to the "submerged
tenth," and to evince a disposition to fulfil it, the
family claim is strenuously asserted; she is told
that she is unjustified, ill-advised in her efforts.
If she persists the family too often are injured and
unhappy, unless the efforts are called missionary,
and the religious zeal of the family carry them
over their sense of abuse. When this zeal does
not exist the result is perplexing. It is a curious
violation of what we would fain believe a fundamental law — that the final return of the Deed is
upon the head of the Doer. The Deed is that of
exclusiveness and caution, but the return instead
of falling upon the head of the exclusive and cau-
tious, falls upon a young head full of generous
and unselfish plans. The girl loses something
vital out of her life which she is entitled to. She
is restricted and unhappy; her elders, meanwhile,
are unconscious of the situation, and we have all
the elements of a tragedy.

We have in America a fast-growing number of cultivated young people who have no recognized outlet for their active faculties. They hear constantly of the great social mal-adjustment, but no way is provided for them to change it, and their uselessness hangs about them heavily. Huxley declares that the sense of uselessness is the severest shock which the human system can sustain, and that, if persistently sustained, it results in atrophy of function. These young people have had advantages of college, of European travel and economic study, but they are sustaining this shock of inaction. They have pet phrases, and they tell you that the things that make us all alike are stronger than the things that make us different. They say that all men are united by needs and sympathies far more permanent and radical than anything that temporarily divides them and sets them in opposition to each other. If they affect art, they say that the decay in artistic expression is due to the decay in ethics, that art when shut away from the human interests and from the great mass of humanity is self-destructive. They tell their elders with all the bitterness of youth that if they expect success from them in business, or politics, or in whatever lines their ambition for them has run, they must let them consult all of humanity; that they must let them find out what the people want and how they want it. It is only the stronger young people, however, who formulate this. Many

of them dissipate their energies in so-called enjoyment.   Others, not content with that, go on studying and go back to college for their second degrees,
not that they are especially fond of study, but because they want something definite to do, and their
powers have been trained in the direction of mental accumulation.   Many are buried beneath mere
mental accumulation with lowered vitality and dis-
content.   Walter Besant says they have had the
vision that Peter had when he saw the great sheet
let down from heaven, wherein was neither clean
nor unclean.   He calls it the sense of humanity.
It is not philanthropy nor benevolence.   It is a
thing fuller and wider than either of these.   This
young life, so sincere in its emotion and good
phrases and yet so undirected, seems to me as
pitiful as the other great mass of destitute lives.
One is supplementary to the other, and some
method of communication can surely be devised.
Mr. Barnett, who urged the first Settlement, —
Toynbee Hall, in East London, — recognized this
need of outlet for the young men of Oxford and
Cambridge, and hoped that the Settlement would
supply the communication.   It is easy to see why
the Settlement movement originated in England,
where the years of education are more constrained
and definite than they are here, where class distinctions are more rigid.   The necessity of it was
greater there, but we are fast feeling the pressure
of the need and meeting the necessity for Settle-

ments in America. Our young people feel nervously the need of putting theory into action, and respond quickly to the Settlement form of activity.

The third division of motives which I believe make toward the Settlement is the result of a certain *renaissance* going forward in Christianity. The impulse to share the lives of the poor, the desire to make social service, irrespective of propaganda, express the spirit of Christ, is as old as Christianity itself. We have no proof from the records themselves that the early Roman Christians, who strained their simple art to the point of grotesqueness in their eagerness to record a "good news" on the walls of the catacombs, considered this "good news" a religion. Jesus had no set of truths labelled "Religious." On the contrary, his doctrine was that all truth is one, that the appropriation of it is freedom. His teaching had no dogma to mark it off from truth and action in general. He himself called it a revelation — a life. These early Roman Christians received the Gospel message, a command to love all men, with a certain joyous simplicity. The image of the Good Shepherd is blithe and gay beyond the gentlest shepherd of Greek mythology; the hart no longer pants, but rushes to the water brooks. The Christians looked for the continuous revelation, but believed what Jesus said, that this revelation to be held and made manifest must be put into terms of action; that action is the only medium man has for receiving and appropriating truth. "If any man will do His will, he shall know of the doctrine."

That Christianity has to be revealed and embodied in the line of social progress is a corollary to the simple proposition that man's action is found in his social relationships in the way in which he connects with his fellows, that his motives for action are the zeal and affection with which he regards his fellows. By this simple process was created a deep enthusiasm for humanity, which regarded man as at once the organ and object of revelation; and by this process came about that wonderful fellowship, that true democracy of the early Church, that so captivates the imagination. The early Christians were pre-eminently non-resistant. They believed in love as a cosmic force. There was no iconoclasm during the minor peace of the Church. They did not yet denounce, nor tear down temples, nor preach the end of the world. They grew to a mighty number, but it never occurred to them, either in their weakness or their strength, to regard other men for an instant as their foes or as aliens. The spectacle of the Christians loving all men was the most astounding Rome had ever seen. They were eager to sacrifice themselves for the weak, for children and the aged. They identified themselves with slaves and did not avoid the plague. They longed to share the common lot that they might receive the constant revelation. It was a new treasure which the early Christians added to the sum of all treasures, a joy hitherto unknown in the world — the joy of finding the Christ which lieth in each man, but which no man can unfold save in fellowship. A happiness ranging from the heroic to the pastoral enveloped them. They were to possess a revelation as long as life had new meaning to unfold, new action to propose.

I believe that there is a distinct turning among many young men and women toward this simple acceptance of Christ's message. They resent the assumption that Christianity is a set of ideas which belong to the religious consciousness, whatever that may be, that it is a thing to be proclaimed and instituted apart from the social life of the community. They insist that it shall seek a simple and natural expression in the social organism itself. The Settlement movement is only one manifestation of that wider humanitarian movement which throughout Christendom, but pre-eminently in England, is endeavoring to embody itself, not in a sect, but in society itself. Tolstoï has reminded us all very forcibly of Christ's principle of non-resistance. His formulation has been startling and his expression has deviated from the general movement, but there is little doubt that he has many adherents, men and women who are philosophically convinced of the futility of opposition, who believe that evil can be overcome only with good and cannot be opposed. If love is the creative force of the universe, the principle which binds men together, and by their interdependence on each other makes them human, just so surely is anger and the spirit of opposition the destructive principle of the universe, that which tears down, thrusts men apart, and makes them isolated and brutal.

I cannot, of course, speak for other Settlements, but it would, I think, be unfair to Hull House not to emphasize the conviction with which the first residents went there, that it would simply be a foolish and an unwarrantable expenditure of force to oppose or to antagonize any individual or set of people in the neighborhood; that whatever of good the House had to offer should be put into positive terms; that its residents should live with opposition to no man, with recognition of the good in every man, even the meanest. I believe that this turning, this *renaissance* of the early Christian humanitarianism, is going on in America, in Chicago, if you please, without leaders who write or philosophize, without much speaking, but with a bent to express in social service, in terms of action, the spirit of Christ. Certain it is that spiritual force is found in the Settlement movement, and it is also true that this force must be evoked and must be called into play before the success of any Settlement is assured. There must be the over-mastering belief that all that is noblest in life is common to men as men, in order to accentuate the likenesses and ignore the differences which are found among the people whom the Settlement constantly brings into juxtaposition. It may be true, as Frederic Harrison insists, that the very religious fervor of man can be turned into love for his race and his desire for a future life into content to live in the echo of his deeds. How far the Positivists' formula of the high ardor for humanity can carry the Settlement movement, Mrs. Humphry Ward's house in London may in course of time illustrate. Paul's formula of seeking for the Christ which lieth in each man and founding our likenesses on him seems a simpler formula to many of us.

If you have heard a thousand voices singing in the Hallelujah Chorus in Handel's " Messiah," you have found that the leading voices could still be distinguished, but that the differences of training and cultivation between them and the voices of the chorus were lost in the unity of purpose and the fact that they were all human voices lifted by a high motive. This is a weak illustration of what a Settlement attempts to do. It aims, in a measure, to lead whatever of social life its neighborhood may afford, to focus and give form to that life, to bring to bear upon it the results of cultivation and training ; but it receives in exchange for the music of isolated voices the volume and strength of the chorus. It is quite impossible for me to say in what proportion or degree the subjective necessity which led to the opening of Hull House combined the three trends: first the desire to interpret democracy in social terms; secondly, the impulse beating at the very source of our lives urging us to aid in the race progress; and, thirdly, the Christian movement toward Humanitarianism. It is difficult to analyze a living thing; the analysis is at best imperfect. Many more motives may blend with the three trends; possibly the desire for a new form of social success due to the nicety of imagination, which refuses worldly pleasures unmixed with the joys of self-sacrifice; possibly a love of approbation, so vast that is it not content with the treble clapping of delicate hands, but wishes also to hear the bass notes from toughened palms, may mingle with these.

The Settlement, then, is an experimental effort to aid in the solution of the social and industrial problems which are engendered by the modern conditions of life in a great city. It insists that these problems are not confined to any one portion of a city. It is an attempt to relieve, at the same time, the over-accumulation at one end of society and the destitution at the other; but it assumes that this over-accumulation and destitution is most sorely felt in the things that pertain to social and educational advantage. From its very nature it can stand for no political or social *propaganda*. It must, in a sense, give the warm welcome of an inn to all such *propaganda*, if perchance one of them be found an angel. The one thing to be dreaded in the Settlement is that it lose its flexibility, its power of quick adaptation, its readiness to change its methods as its environment may demand. It must be open to conviction and must have a deep and abiding sense of tolerance. It must be hospitable and ready for experiment. It should demand from its residents a scientific patience in the accumulation of facts and the steady holding of their sympathies as one of the best instruments for that accumulation. It must be grounded in a philosophy whose foundation is on the solidarity of the human race, a philosophy which will not waver when the race happens to be represented by a drunken woman or an idiot boy. Its residents must be emptied of all conceit of opinion and all self-assertion, and ready to arouse and interpret the public opinion of their neighborhood. They must be content to live quietly side by side with their neighbors until they grow into a sense of relationship and mutual interests. Their neighbors are held apart by differences of race and language which the residents can more easily overcome. They are bound to see the needs of their neighborhood as a whole, to furnish data for legislation, and use their influence to secure it. In short, residents are pledged to devote themselves to the duties of good citizenship and to the arousing of the social energies which too largely lie dormant in every neighborhood given over to industrialism. They are bound to regard the entire life of their city as organic, to make an effort to unify it, and to protest against its over-differentiation.

Our philanthropies of all sorts are growing so
expensive and institutional that it is to be hoped
the Settlement movement will keep itself facile
and unincumbered. From its very nature it needs
no endowment, no roll of salaried officials. Many
residents must always come in the attitude of students, assuming that the best teacher of life is life
itself, and regarding the Settlement as a class-
room. Hull House from the outside may appear
to be a cumbrous plant of manifold industries,
with its round of clubs and classes, its day nursery,
diet kitchen, library, art exhibits, lectures, statistical work and polyglot demands for information,
a thousand people coming and going in an average
week. But viewed as a business enterprise it is
not costly, for from this industry are eliminated
two great items of expense — the cost of superin-
tendence and the cost of distribution. All the
management and teaching are voluntary and un-
paid, and the consumers — to continue the commercial phraseology — are at the door and deliver
the goods themselves. In the instance of Hull
House, rent is also largely eliminated through the
courtesy of the owner.

Life is manifold and Hull House attempts to
respond to as many sides as possible. It does this
fearlessly, feeling sure that among the able people
of Chicago are those who will come to do the work
when once the outline is indicated. It pursues
much the same policy in regard to money. It

seems to me an advantage — this obligation to appeal to business men for their judgment and their money, to the educated for their effort and enthusiasm, to the neighborhood for their response and co-operation. It tests the sanity of an idea, and we enter upon a new line of activity with a feeling of support and confidence. We have always been perfectly frank with our neighbors. I have never tried so earnestly to set forth the gist of the Settlement movement, to make clear its reciprocity, as I have to them. At first we were often asked why we came to live there when we could afford to live somewhere else. I remember one man who used to shake his head and say it was "the strangest thing he had met in his experience," but who was finally convinced that it was not strange but natural. I trust that now it seems natural to all of us that the Settlement should be there. If it is natural to feed the hungry and care for the sick, it is certainly natural to give pleasure to the young and to minister to the deep-seated craving for social intercourse that all men feel. Whoever does it is rewarded by something which, if not gratitude, is at least spontaneous and vital and lacks that irksome sense of obligation with which a substantial benefit is too often acknowledged. The man who looks back to the person who first put him in the way of good literature has no alloy in his gratitude.

I remember when the statement seemed to me

very radical that the salvation of East London was
the destruction of West London; but I believe now
that there will be no wretched quarters in our cities
at all when the conscience of each man is so touched
that he prefers to live with the poorest of his breth-
ren, and not with the richest of them that his income will allow. It is to be hoped that this moving
and living will at length be universal and need no
name. The Settlement movement is from its
nature a provisional one. It is easy in writing a
paper to make all philosophy point one particular
moral and all history adorn one particular tale;
but I hope you forgive me for reminding you that
the best speculative philosophy sets forth the
solidarity of the human race; that the highest
moralists have taught that without the advance
and improvement of the whole no man can hope
for any lasting improvement in his own moral
or material individual condition. The subjective
necessity for Social Settlements is identical with
that necessity which urges us on toward social and
individual salvation.

II.

THE OBJECTIVE VALUE OF A SOCIAL SETTLE-- MENT.

By Jane Addams, "Hull House," Chicago.

In treating of the value of the Social Settlement, I shall confine myself to Hull House, and
what it has been able to do for its neighborhood,
only because I am most familiar with that Settlement.

Hull House stands on South Halsted Street,
next door to the corner of Polk. South Halsted
Street is thirty-two miles long and one of the
great thoroughfares of Chicago. Polk Street
crosses Halsted midway between the stock-yards
to the south and the ship-building yards on the
north branch of the Chicago River. For the six
miles between these two industries the street is
lined with shops of butchers and grocers, with
dingy and gorgeous saloons, and pretentious establishments for the sale of ready-made clothing.
Polk Street, running west from Halsted Street,
grows rapidly more respectable; running a mile
east to State Street, it grows steadily worse, and
crosses a net-work of gilded vice on the corners of
Clark Street and Fourth Avenue.

Hull House is an ample old residence, well built and somewhat ornately decorated after the manner of its time, 1856. It has been used for many purposes, and although battered by its vicissitudes, is essentially sound and has responded kindly to repairs and careful furnishing. Its wide hall and open fires always insure it a gracious aspect. It once stood in the suburbs, but the city has steadily grown up around it and its site now has corners on three or four more or less distinct foreign colonies. Between Halsted Street and the river live about ten thousand Italians : Neapolitans, Sicilians, and Calabrians, with an occasional Lombard or Venetian. To the south on Twelfth Street are many Germans, and side streets are given over almost entirely to Polish and Russian Jews. Still farther south, these Jewish colonies merge into a huge Bohemian colony, so vast that Chicago ranks as the third Bohemian city in the world. To the northwest are many Canadian-French, clannish in spite of their long residence in America, and to the north are many Irish and first-generation Americans. On the streets directly west and farther north are well-to-do English-speaking families, many of whom own their houses and have lived in the neighborhood for years. I know one man who is still living in his old farm-house. This corner of Polk and Halsted Streets is in the fourteenth precinct of the nineteenth ward. This ward has a population of about fifty thousand, and at the last presidential election registered 7072 voters. It has had no unusual political scandal connected with it, but its aldermen are generally saloon-keepers and its political manipulations are those to be found in the crowded wards where the activities of the petty politician are unchecked.

The policy of the public authorities of never taking an initiative, and always waiting to be urged to do their duty, is fatal in a ward where there is no initiative among the citizens. The idea underlying our self-government breaks down in such a ward. The streets are inexpressibly dirty, the number of schools inadequate, factory legislation unenforced, the street-lighting bad, the paving miserable and altogether lacking in the alleys and smaller streets, and the stables defy all laws of sanitation. Hundreds of houses are unconnected with the street sewer. The older and richer inhabitants seem anxious to move away as rapidly as they can afford it. They make room for newly arrived immigrants who are densely ignorant of civic duties. This substitution of the older inhabitants is accomplished industrially also in the south and east quarters of the ward. The Hebrews and Italians do the finishing for the great clothing-manufacturers formerly done by Americans, Irish, and Germans, who refused to submit to the extremely low prices to which the sweating system has reduced their successors. As the design of the sweating system is the elimination of rent from the manufacture of

clothing, the "outside work" is begun after the
clothing leaves the cutter. An unscrupulous con-
tractor regards no basement as too dark, no stable
loft too foul, no rear shanty too provisional, no
tenement room too small for his workroom, as
these conditions imply low rental. Hence these
shops abound in the worst of the foreign districts,
where the sweater easily finds his cheap basement
and his home finishers. There is a constant tendency to employ school-children, as much of the
home and shop work can easily be done by children.

The houses of the ward, for the most part wooden,
were originally built for one family and are now
occupied by several. They are after the type of
the inconvenient frame cottages found in the
poorer suburbs twenty years ago. Many of them
were built where they now stand; others were
brought thither on rollers, because their previous
site had been taken for a factory. The fewer brick
tenement buildings which are three or four stories
high are comparatively new. There are few huge
and foul tenements. The little wooden houses
have a temporary aspect, and for this reason, perhaps, the tenement-house legislation in Chicago
is totally inadequate. Back tenements flourish;
many houses have no water supply save the faucet
in the back yard; there are no fire escapes; the
garbage and ashes are placed in wooden boxes
which are fastened to the street pavements. One
of the most discouraging features about the present

system of tenement houses is that many are owned by sordid and ignorant immigrants. The theory that wealth brings responsibility, that possession entails at length education and refinement, in these cases fails utterly. The children of an Italian immigrant owner do not go to school and are no improvement on their parents. His wife picks rags from the street gutter, and laboriously sorts them in a dingy court. Wealth may do something for her self-complacency and feeling of consequence ; it certainly does nothing for her comfort or her children's improvement nor for the cleanliness of any one concerned. Another thing that prevents better houses in Chicago is the tentative attitude of the real-estate men. Many unsavory conditions are allowed to continue which would be regarded with horror if they were considered permanent. Meanwhile, the wretched conditions persist until at least two generations of children have been born and reared in them.

Our ward contains two hundred and fifty-five saloons; our own precinct boasts of eight, and the one directly north of us twenty. This allows one saloon to every twenty-eight voters, and there is no doubt that the saloon is the centre of the liveliest political and social life of the ward. The leases and fixtures of these saloons are, in the majority of cases, owned by the wholesale liquor houses, and the saloon-keeper himself is often a bankrupt.

There are seven churches and two missions in the ward. All of these are small and somewhat struggling, save the large Catholic church connected with the Jesuit College on the south boundary of the ward, and the French Catholic church on the west boundary. Out of these nine religious centres there are but three in which the service is habitually conducted in English. This enumeration of churches does not include the chevras found among the recently immigrated Jews of the Ashkenazite branch. The chevras combine the offices of public worship and the rites of mourning with the function of a sick benefit and mutual aid society. There are seven Catholic parochial schools in the ward, accommodating 6244 children; three Protestant schools care for 141 children. A fine manual-training school sustained by the Hebrews is found in the seventh ward just south of us. In the same ward is the receiving shelter for the Jewish refugees.

This site for a Settlement was selected in the first instance because of its diversity and the variety of activity for which it presented an opportunity. It has been the aim of the residents to respond to all sides of the neighborhood life: not to the poor people alone, nor to the well-to-do, nor to the young in contradistinction to the old, but to the neighborhood as a whole, "men, women, and children taken in families as the Lord mixes them." The activities of Hull House divide themselves into four, possibly more lines. They are not formally or consciously thus divided, but broadly separate according to the receptivity of the neighbors. They might be designated as the social, educational, and humanitarian, I have added civic — if indeed a Settlement of women can be said to perform civic duties. These activities spring from no preconceived notion of what a Social Settlement should be, but have increased gradually on demand. In describing these activities and their value to the neighborhood, I shall attempt to identify those people who respond to each form.

A Settlement which regards social intercourse as the terms of its expression logically brings to its aid all those adjuncts which have been found by experience to free social life. It casts aside nothing which the cultivated man regards as good and suggestive of participation in the best life of the past. It ignores none of the surroundings which one associates with a life of simple refinement. The amount of luxury which an individual indulges in is a thing which has to be determined by each for himself. It must always be a relative thing. The one test which the Settlement is bound to respect is that its particular amount of luxury shall tend to "free" the social expression of its neighbors, and not cumber that expression. The residents at Hull House find that the better in quality and taste their surroundings are, the more they contribute to the general enjoyment.

We have distinct advantages for Settlements in America. There are fewer poor people here than in England, there are fewer poor people who expect to remain poor, and they are less strictly confined to their own districts. It is an advantage that our cities are diversified by foreign colonies. We go to Europe and consider our view incomplete if we do not see something of the peasant life of the little villages with their quaint customs and suggestive habits. We can see the same thing here. There are Bohemians, Italians, Poles, Russians, Greeks, and Arabs in Chicago vainly trying to adjust their peasant life to the life of a large city, and coming in contact with only the most ignorant Americans in that city. The more of scholarship, the more of linguistic attainment, the more of beautiful surroundings a Settlement among them can command, the more it can do for them.

It is much easier to deal with the first generation of crowded city life than with the second or third, because it is more natural and cast in a simpler mould. The Italian and Bohemian peasants who live in Chicago still put on their bright holiday clothes on a Sunday and go to visit their cousins. They tramp along with at least a suggestion of having once walked over ploughed fields and breathed country air. The second generation of city poor have no holiday clothes and consider their cousins " a bad lot." I have heard a drunken man, in a maudlin stage, babble of his good country mother and imagine he was driving the cows home, and I knew that his little son, who laughed loud at him, would be drunk earlier in life, and would have no such pastoral interlude to his ravings. Hospitality still survives among foreigners, although it is buried under false pride among the poorest Americans. One thing seemed clear in regard to entertaining these foreigners : to preserve and keep for them whatever of value their past life contained and to bring them in contact with a better type of Americans. For two years, every Saturday evening, our Italian neighbors were our guests; entire families came. These evenings were very popular during our first winter at Hull House. Many educated Italians helped us, and the house became known as a place where Italians were welcome and where national holidays were observed. They come to us with their petty lawsuits, sad relics of the *vendetta*, with their incorrigible boys, with their hospital cases, with their aspirations for American clothes, and with their needs for an interpreter.

Friday evening is devoted to Germans and is similar in purpose ; but owing to the superior education of our Teutonic guests and the clever leading of a cultivated German woman, we can bring out the best of that cozy social intercourse which is found in its perfection in the " Fatherland." They sing a great deal in the tender minor of the German folksong or in the rousing spirit of the

Rhine, and they are slowly but persistently pursuing a course in German history and literature. The relationship by no means ends with social civilities, and the acquaintance made there has brought about radical changes in the lives of many friendless families. I recall one peasant woman, straight from the fields of Germany. Her two years in America had been spent in patiently carrying water up and down two flights of stairs, and in washing the heavy flannel suits of iron-foundry workers. For this her pay had averaged thirty-five cents a day. Three of her daughters had fallen victims to the vice of the city. The mother was bewildered and distressed, but understood nothing. We were able to induce the betrayer of one daughter to marry her; the second, after a tedious lawsuit, supported his child; with the third we were able to do nothing. This woman is now living with her family in a little house seventeen miles from the city. She has made two payments on her land and is a lesson to all beholders as she pastures her cow up and down the railroad tracks and makes money from her ten acres. She did not need charity. She had an immense capacity for hard work, but she sadly needed "heading." She is our most shining example, but I think of many forlorn cases of German and Bohemian peasants in need of neighborly help.

Perhaps of more value than to the newly arrived

peasant is the service of the Settlement to those foreigners who speak English fairly well, and who have been so successful in material affairs that they are totally absorbed by them. Their social life is too often reduced to a sense of comradeship. The lives of many Germans, for instance, are law-abiding, but inexpressibly dull. They have resigned poetry and romance with the other good things of the Fatherland. There is a strong family affection between them and their English-speaking children, but their pleasures are not in common and they seldom go out together. Perhaps the greatest value of the Settlement to them is in simply plac-ing large and pleasant rooms with musical facili-ties at their disposal, and in reviving their almost forgotten enthusiasm for Körner and Schiller. I have seen sons and daughters stand in complete surprise as their mother's knitting-needles softly beat time to the song she was singing, or her worn face turned rosy under the hand-clapping as she made an old-fashioned courtesy at the end of a German poem. It was easy to fancy a growing touch of respect in her children's manner to her, and a rising enthusiasm for German literature and reminiscence on the part of all the family, an effort to bring together the old life and the new, a respect for the older cultivation, and not quite so much assurance that the new was the best. I think that we have a right to expect that our foreigners will do this for us: that they will project a little of the historic and romantic into the prosaic quarters of our American cities.

But our social evenings are by no means confined to foreigners. Our most successful clubs are entirely composed of English-speaking and American-born young people. Those over sixteen meet in two clubs, one for young men and one for girls, every Monday evening. Each club dispatches various literary programs before nine o'clock, when they meet together for an hour of social amusement before going home at ten. The members of the Tuesday evening clubs are from fourteen to sixteen years old; a few of them are still in school, but most of them are working. The boys who are known as the Young Citizen's Club are supposed to inform themselves on municipal affairs, as are the Hull House Columbian Guards who report alleys and streets for the Municipal Order League. We have various other clubs of young people that meet weekly; their numbers are limited only by the amount of room. We hold the dining-room, the reception-room, and the octagon with the art-exhibit-room and the studio each evening for the College Extension classes, and can reserve only the large drawing-room and gymnasium for the clubs and receptions. The gymnasium is a somewhat pretentious name for a building next door which was formerly a saloon, but which we rented last fall, repaired, and fitted up with good apparatus. A large and well-

equipped gymnasium is at present being built
for Hull House. During the winter the old one
sheltered some enthusiastic athletic classes. The
evenings were equally divided between men and
women. The children came in the afternoon. It
is difficult to describe the social evenings, and
there is much social life going on constantly which
cannot be tabulated.

To turn to the educational effort, it will be perhaps better first to describe the people who respond
to it. In every neighborhood where poorer people
live, because rents are supposed to be cheaper
there, is an element which, although uncertain in
the individual, in the aggregate can be counted
upon. It is composed of people of former education and opportunity who have cherished ambitions
and prospects, but who are caricatures of what
they meant to be — "hollow ghosts which blame
the living men." There are times in many lives
when there is a cessation of energy and loss of
power. Men and women of education and refinement come to live in a cheaper neighborhood because they lack the power of making money,
because of ill health, because of an unfortunate
marriage, or for various other reasons which do
not imply criminality or stupidity. Among them
are those who, in spite of untoward circumstances,
keep up some sort of an intellectual life, those
who are "great for books" as their neighbors say.
To such the Settlement is a genuine refuge. In

addition to these there are many young women
who teach in the public schools, young men who
work at various occupations, but who are bent
upon self-improvement and are preparing for professions. It is of these that the College Extension
classes are composed. The majority of the two
hundred students live within the radius of six
blocks from the house, although a few of them
come from other parts of the city. The educational effort of Hull House always has been held
by the residents to be subordinate to its social life,
and, as it were, a part of it. What is now known
as the College Extension course, a series of lectures
and classes held in the evening on the general
plan of University Extension, had its origin in an
informal club which, during the first winter, read
" Romola " with the original residents. During
the last term thirty-five classes a week were in
existence. The work is divided into terms of
twelve weeks, and circulars are issued at the
beginning of each term. Many students have
taken studies in each of the seven terms of work
offered.

The relation of students and faculty to each
other and to the residents is that of guest and
hostess, and those students who have been longest
in relation to the Settlement feel the responsibility
of old friends of the house to new guests. A good
deal of tutoring is constantly going on among the
students themselves in the rooms of Hull House.

At the close of each term the residents give a reception to students and faculty, which is one of the chief social events of the season. Upon this comfortable social basis very good work has been done in the College Extension courses. Literature classes until recently have been the most popular. The last winter's Shakespeare class had a regular attendance of forty. The mathematical classes have always been large and flourishing. The faculty, consisting of college men and women, numbers thirty-five. Many of them have taught constantly at the house for two years, but their numbers are often re-enforced. During the last term a class in physics, preparatory for a class in electricity, was composed largely of workmen in the Western Electric Works, which are within a few blocks of Hull House. A fee of fifty cents is charged for each course of study. This defrays all incidental expenses and leaves on hand each term fifty or seventy dollars, with which to import distinguished lecturers.

During the last winter Hull House has been a successful "centre" for two University Extension courses in connection with the Chicago University. It has always been the policy of Hull House to co-operate as much as possible with public institutions. The Chicago Public Library has an almost unique system of branch reading-rooms and library stations. Five rooms are rented by the library in various parts of the city which are fitted up for

reading-rooms, and in addition to magazines and
papers they are supplied with several hundred
books. There are also other stations where public-
library cards can be left and to which books are
delivered. Hull House was made one of these
delivery stations during its second year, and when
in June, 1891, the Butler Gallery was completed,
we offered the lower floor free of rent as a branch
reading-room. The City Library supplies English
magazines and papers and two librarians who are
in charge. There are papers in Italian, German,
Bohemian, and French. The number of readers
the first month was 1213; during the fifth month,
2454. The upper floor of the Butler Gallery is
divided into an art exhibition room and a studio.
Our first art exhibit was opened in June, 1891, by
Mr. and Mrs. Barnett, of St. Jude's, Whitechapel.
It is always pleasant to associate their hearty sympathy with that first exhibit. The pictures were
some of the best that Chicago could afford, several
by Corot, Watts, and Davis. European country
scenes, sea views, and Dutch interiors bring forth
many pleasant reminiscences, and the person who
is in charge of the pictures to explain them is
many times more edified than edifying. We have
had five exhibits since the gallery was completed,
two of oil-paintings, one of old engravings and etch-
ings, one of water-colors, and one of pictures especially selected for use in the public schools. The
average attendance at these exhibits has been

three thousand. An exhibit is open from two in the afternoon until ten in the evening, and continues usually two weeks. The value of these exhibits to the neighborhood must, of course, be determined by the value one attaches to the sense of beauty and the pleasure which arises from its contemplation. Classes in free-hand drawing and clay modelling are held in the studio of the Butler Gallery. They have been very popular from the first, and some excellent work has been done.

Every Thursday evening for three years, save during the three summer months, we have had a lecture of some sort at Hull House. This has come to be an expected event in the neighborhood. These lectures are largely attended by the College Extension students, and the topics are supposed to connect with their studies; but many other people come to them and often join a a class because of the interest a lecturer has awakened. This attraction is constantly in mind when these lectures are planned. For two years a summer school has been held at Rockford, Ill., in connection with the College Extension classes. From one-third to one-half the students have been able to attend it, paying their board for a month, and enjoying out-door study quite as much as the classes. I would recommend for imitation the very generous action on the part of the Rockford College trustees in placing at our disposal free of rent their entire educational apparatus, from the

dining-room to the laboratories. On the border
land between social and educational activity are
our Sunday afternoon concerts, and the Plato Club
which follows them.

The industrial education of Hull House has
always been somewhat limited. From the beginning we have had large and enthusiastic cooking
classes, first in the Hull House kitchen, and later
in a tiny cottage across the yard which has been
fitted up for the purpose. We have also always
had sewing, mending, and embroidery classes.
This leads me to speak of the children who meet
weekly at Hull House, whose organization is between classes and clubs. There are three hundred
of them who come on three days, not counting, of
course, the children who come to the house merely
as depositors in the Penny Provident Fund Savings
Bank. A hundred Italian girls come on Monday.
They sew and carry home a new garment, which
becomes a pattern for the entire family. Tuesday
afternoon has always been devoted to school-boys'
clubs: they are practically story-telling clubs. The
most popular stories are legends and tales of chivalry. The one hundred and fifty little girls on
Friday afternoon are not very unlike the boys,
although they want to sew while they are hearing
their stories. The value of these clubs, I believe,
lies almost entirely in their success in arousing
the higher imagination. We have had a kindergarten at Hull House ever since we have lived

there. Every morning miniature Italians, Hebrews, French, Irish, and Germans assemble in our drawing-room, and nothing seems to excite admiration in the neighborhood so much as the fact that we "put up with them."

In addition to the neighbors who respond to the receptions and classes are found those who are too battered and oppressed to care for them. To these, however, is left that susceptibility to the bare offices of humanity which raises such offices into a bond of fellowship. These claim humanitarian efforts. Perhaps the chief value of a Settlement to its neighborhood, certainly to the newly arrived foreigner, is its office as an information and interpretation bureau. It sometimes seems as if the business of the Settlement were that of a commission merchant. Without endowment and without capital itself, it constantly acts between the various institutions of the city and the people for whose benefit these institutions were erected. The hospitals, the county agencies, and State asylums, are often but vague rumors to the people who need them most. This commission work, as I take it, is of value not only to the recipient, but to the institutions themselves. Each institution, unlike a settlement, is obliged to determine upon the line of its activity, to accept its endowment for that end and do the best it can. But each time this is accomplished it is apt to lace itself up in certain formulas, is in danger of forgetting the mystery

and complexity of life, of repressing the prompt-
ings that spring from growing insight.

The residents of a Social Settlement have an
opportunity of seeing institutions from the recipient's standpoint, of catching the spirit of the original impulse which founded them. This experience
ought to have a certain value and ultimately find
expression in institutional management. One of
the residents of Hull House received this winter
an appointment from the Cook County agent as a
county visitor. She reported at the agency each
morning, and all the cases within a radius of several blocks from Hull House were given to her for
investigation. This gave her a legitimate opportunity for knowing the poorest people in the neighborhood. In no cases were her recommendations
refused or her judgments reversed by the men in
charge of the office. From the very nature of our
existence and purpose we are bound to keep on
good terms with every beneficent institution in the
city. Passing by our telephone last Sunday morning, I was struck with the list of numbers hung on
the wall for easy reference. They were those of
the Visiting Nurses' Association; Cook County
Hospital; Women's and Children's Hospital; Max-
well Street Police Station for city ambulance;
Health Department, City Hall; Cook County
Agent, etc. We have been on very good terms
with the Hebrew Relief and Aid Society, the Children's Aid, the Humane Society, the Municipal

Order League, and with the various church and national relief associations. Every summer we send out dozens of children to the country on the " Daily News " Fresh Air Fund and to the Holiday Home at Lake Geneva. Our most complete co-operation has been with the Visiting Nurses' Association. One of the nurses lives at Hull House, pays her board as a resident, and does her work from there. Friends of the house are constantly in need of her ministrations, and her cases become friends of the house. Owing to the lack of a charity organization society in Chicago we have been obliged to keep a sum of money as a relief fund. Five bath-rooms in the rear of Hull House are open to the neighborhood and are constantly in use. The number of baths taken in July was nine hundred and eighty.

The more definite humanitarian effort of Hull House has taken shape in a day nursery, which was started during the second year of our residence on Halsted Street. A frame cottage of six rooms across our yard has been fitted up as a *crèche*. At present we receive from thirty to forty children daily. A young lady who has had kindergarten training is in charge ; she has the assistance of an older woman, and a kindergarten by a professional teacher is held each morning in the play-room. This nursery is not merely a convenience in the neighborhood ; it is, to a certain extent, a neighborhood affair. Similar in spirit is the Hull House

Diet Kitchen, in a little cottage directly back of the nursery. Food is prepared for invalids and orders are taken from physicians and visiting nurses of the district. We have lately had an outfit of Mr. Atkinson's inventions, in which the women of the neighborhood have taken a most intelligent interest, especially the members of the Hull House Woman's Club. This club meets one afternoon a week. It is composed of the most able women of the neighborhood, who enjoy the formal addresses and many informal discussions. The economics of food and fuel are freely discussed. The Hull House household expenses are frankly compared with those of other households. There is little doubt that "friendly visiting," while of great value, to be complete should also include the "friendly visited." The residents at Hull House find in themselves a constantly increasing tendency to consult their neighbors on the advisability of each new undertaking. We have lately opened a boarding club for working girls near Hull House on the co-operative plan. I say advisedly that we have "opened" it; the running of it is quite in the hands of the girls themselves. The furniture, pictures, etc., belong to Hull House, and whatever experience we have is at their disposal; but it is in no sense a working-girls' "home," nor is it to be run from the outside. We hope a great deal from this little attempt at co-operative housekeeping. The club has been running three months on a self-supporting basis and has thirty-five members.

The Coffee House which is being built in connection with Hull House contains a large kitchen fitted on the New-England Kitchen plan. We hope by the sale of properly cooked foods, to make not only co-operative housekeeping but all the housekeeping of the neighborhood easier and more economical. The Coffee House itself, with its club-rooms, will be a less formal social centre than our drawing-room.

Helpful recourses from the neighborhood itself constantly develop, physicians benefit societies, ministers and priests are always ready to co-operate in any given case. Young girls from the neighborhood assist in the children's classes, mothers help in the nursery, young men teach in the gymnasium, or secure students for an experimental course of lectures. We constantly rely more and more on neighborhood assistance.

In summing up the objective value of Hull House, I am sorry we have not more to present in the line of civic activities. It was through the energy of a resident this spring that the fact that the public-school census recorded 6976 school-children in the nineteenth ward and that they were provided with only 2957 public-school sittings was made prominent just before the appropriations were voted for school buildings and sites. It was largely through her energy, and the energy of the people whom she interested in it, that the Board of Education was induced to purchase a site for a school building in our ward and to save and equip for immediate use a school-house about to be turned into a warehouse.

During two months of this summer the reports sent in from Hull House to the Municipal Order League, and through it to the Health Department, were one thousand and thirty-seven. The Department showed great readiness to co-operate with this volunteer inspection, and a marked improvement has taken place in the scavenger service and in the regulation of the small stables of the ward.

Hull House has had, I hope, a certain value to the women's trades unions of Chicago. It seems to me of great importance that as trades unions of women are being formed they should be kept, if possible, from falling into the self-same pits the men's unions have fallen into. Women possessing no votes, and therefore having little political value, will be both of advantage and disadvantage to their unions. Four women's unions have met regularly at Hull House: the book-binders', the shoemakers', the shirtmakers', and the cloak-makers'. The last two were organized at Hull House. It has seemed to us that the sewing trades are most in need of help. They are thoroughly disorganized, Russian and Polish tailors competing against English-speaking tailors, young girls and Italian women competing against both. An efficient union which should combine all these elements seems very difficult, unless it grow strong enough to offer a label and receive unexpected aid from the manufacturers. In that case there would be the hope of co-operation on the part of the consumers, as the fear of contagion from ready-made clothing has at last seized the imagination of the public.

That the trades unions themselves care for what we have done for them, is shown by the fact that when the committee of investigation for the sweating system was appointed by the Trades and Labor Assembly, consisting of five delegates from the unions and five from other citizens, two of the latter were residents of Hull House. It is logical that a Settlement should have a certain value in labor complications, having from its very position sympathies entangled on both sides. Last May twenty girls from a knitting factory who struck because they were docked for loss of time when they were working by the piece, came directly from the factory to Hull House. They had heard that we "stood by working people." We were able to have the strike arbitrated, and although six girls lost their places, the unjust fines were remitted, and we had the satisfaction of putting on record one more case of arbitration in the slowly growing list. We were helped in this case, as we have been in many others, by the Bureau of Justice. Its office is constantly crowded with working people who hope for redress from the law, but have

no money with which to pay for it.   There should
be an office of this bureau in every ward; "down
town" seems far away and inaccessible to the most
ignorant.   Hull House, in spite of itself, does a
good deal of legal work.   We have secured support
for deserted women, insurance for bewildered wid-
ows, damages for injured operators, furniture from
the clutches of the instalment store.   One function
of the Settlement to its neighborhood somewhat
resembles that of the big brother whose mere presence on the play-ground protects the little one
from bullies.   A resident at Hull House is at
present collecting labor statistics in the neighborhood for the Illinois State Bureau of Labor.   It is
a matter of satisfaction that this work can be done
from the Settlement, and the residents receive the
benefit of the information collected.

It is difficult to classify the Working People's
Social Science Club, which meets weekly at Hull
House.   It is social, educational, and civic in character, the latter chiefly because it strongly connects
the House with the labor problems in their political
and social aspects.   This club was organized at
Hull House in the spring of 1890 by an English
working-man.   It has met weekly since, save during the months of summer.   At eight o'clock every
Wednesday evening the secretary calls to order
from forty to one hundred people.   A chairman
for the evening is elected, and a speaker is intro-
duced who is allowed to talk until nine o'clock;

his subject is then thrown open to discussion and
a lively debate ensues until ten o'clock, at which
hour the meeting is declared adjourned. The enthusiasm of this club seldom lags. Its zest for discussion is unceasing, and any attempt to turn it
into a study or reading club always meets with the
strong disapprobation of the members. Chicago is
full of social theorists. It offers a cosmopolitan
opportunity for discussion. The only possible danger from this commingling of many theories is in-
curred when there is an attempt at suppression;
bottled up, there is danger of explosion; constantly
uncorked, open to the deodorizing and freeing process of the air, all danger is averted. Nothing so
disconcerts a social agitator as to find among his
auditors men who have been through all that, and
who are quite as radical as he in another direction.

The economic conferences which were held between business men and working-men, during the
winter of 1888–89 and the two succeeding winters,
doubtless did much toward relieving this state of
effervescence. Many thoughtful men in Chicago
are convinced that, if these conferences had been
established earlier, the Haymarket riot and all its
sensational results might have been avoided. The
Sunset Club is at present performing much the
same function. There is still need, however, for
many of these clubs where men who differ widely
in their social theories can meet for discussion,
where representatives of the various economic

schools can modify each other, and at least learn
tolerance and the futility of endeavoring to convince all the world of the truth of one position.
To meet in a social-science club is more educational
than to meet in a single-tax club, or a socialistic
chapter, or a personal-rights league, although the
millennium may seem farther off after such a meeting. In addition to this modification of view there
is doubtless a distinct modification of attitude.
Last spring the Hull House Social Science Club
heard a series of talks on municipal and county
affairs by the heads of the various departments.
During the discussion following the address on
"The Chicago Police," a working-man had the
pleasure of telling the chief of police that he had
been arrested, obliged to pay two dollars and a half,
and had lost three days' work, because he had come
out of the wrong gate when he was working on the
World's Fair grounds. The chief sighed, expressed
his regret, and made no defence. The speaker sat
down bewildered; evidently for the first time in
his life he realized that blunders cut the heart of
more than the victim.

Is it possible for men, however far apart in outward circumstances, for the capitalist and the
working-man, to use the common phrase, to meet
as individuals beneath a friendly roof, open their
minds each to each, and not have their "class theories" insensibly modified by the kindly attrition
of a personal acquaintance? In the light of our
experience I should say not,

In describing Hull House and in referring so often to the "residents," I feel that I may have given a wrong impression. By far the larger amount of the teaching and formal club work is done by people living outside of the House. Between ninety and one hundred of these people meet an appointment regularly each week. Our strength lies largely in this element. The average number of people who come to the House during the week is one thousand.

I am always sorry to have Hull House regarded as philanthropy, although it doubtless has strong philanthropic tendencies, and has several distinct charitable departments which are conscientiously carried on. It is unfair, however, to apply the word philanthropic to the activities of the House as a whole. Charles Booth, in his brilliant chapter on "The Unemployed," expresses regret that the problems of the working class are so often confounded with the problems of the inefficient, the idle, and distressed. To confound thus two problems is to render the solution of both impossible. Hull House, while endeavoring to fulfil its obligations to neighbors of varying needs, will do great harm if it confounds distinct problems. Working people live in the same streets with those in need of charity, but they themselves, so long as they have health and good wages, require and want none of it. As one of their number has said, they require only that their aspirations be recognized and stimulated, and the means of attaining them put at their disposal. Hull House makes a constant effort to secure these means for its neighbors, but to call that effort philanthropy is to use the word unfairly and to underestimate the duties of good citizenship.

III.

THE UNIVERSITY SETTLEMENT IDEA.

By Robert A. Woods, "The Andover House," Boston.

In the movement toward a better social life which is going forward nearly everywhere now, there is a resemblance to the great changes that took place at the end of the Middle Ages, out of which came the nations of modern Europe. All Europe had for the time forgotten itself in the excitement and adventure of the Crusades. A new and strange world, with its unusual customs and activities, had come into general knowledge, and began to give men a fresh look at their old surroundings from an altered point of view. A great moral impulse, which united all classes of society, and men from distant places, threw aside the petty rule of feudal lords and made the minds of the people open to the thought of being held together in the larger national bond.

At present we are returning from the modern kind of adventure, — from exploration, enterprise, invention. Applying to the general life of men the new conception of complex and intimate rela-

tionships which the advance of science has brought,
and the idea of unity which is the note of the philosophy of the time, we are working toward vast
changes in the life of modern society, not perhaps
so visible and outward as those involved in the for-
mation of nations, but so profound as to be likely to
make over the inner and closer life of modern people.

The old bond of union was that of a political
compact; the new bond of union is that of a social
organism. It must have seemed difficult enough
for those who had known only loyalty to a local
lord to think of large numbers of duchies being
held together by the single power of one great
ruler; to think of an influence which should per-
meate into the different villages, and bring each
into a common feeling with all the rest. The progress of republican government was held back at
first, and is still greatly hindered, by the feeling
that the people as rulers can wield only an intang-
ible and ineffective force, as against the amorphous
and unwieldy mass of the people as the subjects of
government. But the idea of the nation, and of
the self-governed nation, is now a commonplace;
it is the idea of the social organism that we, in our
turn, are struggling to make real to ourselves.

Civilization is overreaching itself. Certain of
its tendencies develop rankly, before corrective
tendencies have begun to operate. The result is
congestion in some places, and atrophy in others.
We must find ways of uniting the parts of the

social body, under the bonds of civilization, so that its vital influence shall not linger sluggishly at certain centres, but shall run strongly out into every distant extremity. It is no longer the negative ends of safety and freedom that are most to be sought for; it is as to the living out of life among the people that we are concerned. What has been left undone by spent forces will be accomplished through the rising momentum of new forces. We find ourselves compelled, to-day, in the interest of civilization itself, to see that the influences of civilization penetrate into all the ramifications of society. The great city — the typical product of civilization — shows by multiple effects the danger of having people cut off from the better life of society, and breeding with phenomenal rapidity all the evils with which society is cursed. And the difficulty is by no means confined to the most crowded quarters of cities. The poverty of the means of life is felt in other sections of cities besides those called the slums, among grades of people above those called the working people. Factory towns grow quickly, and mass together a large population with very little care that they shall live in a human way. And country villages, cut off by distance from elevating influences, as crowded city quarters are by their numbers, often reached by the bad effects of civilization far more quickly than by the good, offer a problem almost as serious as that of the cities themselves.

This situation, while it has always existed to a degree, is yet distinctly the product of the present time. Not until now could we fairly have appreciated it. Only now have we means adapted to meet it. Only modern civilization could have brought about the difficulty; only modern civilization could have understood it; only modern civilization can overcome it. The task is to make provision so that every part of society shall not only have a full supply for its fundamental human wants, but shall also be constantly refreshed from the higher sources of happier and nobler life. The great social evil is that the resources of society are so illy applied to the supplying of its needs. There must be a shifting of resources to meet needs. The forces of civilization must be mobilized, and made ready for every sort of transference, until every tenement block, every country hamlet, may be able each in its kind to summon for its use all that can push out the present boundaries of life so as to make life what it is designed to be. From the point of view of the individual, and at close range, this is philanthropy; from the point of view of society, this is only far-sighted social statesmanship. The isolated philanthropy of one generation becomes the organized social work of the next, and perhaps the public charge of the third. The moral bullion of one age becomes the economic, and even the political, legal tender of the succeeding age. And these outward changes fully indicate that the new bond of union has been entered into by society; and that in higher and higher ranges of life the forces of civilization are having a way made straight for them; so that more and more the best that life can mean shall become current in the whole experience of men, and shall add some distinctive touch to all their words and acts.

Now, apart from all general movements, political, economic, educational, and religious, toward a more comprehensive and more delicate organization of social life, there is a necessity for work to be done at many points where social evils are intrenched so that they cannot be met, even if they could be rightly estimated, by such agencies. The arm of the law, public and private charity, benevolent societies and institutions, churches, may fulfil ever so well their particular functions; but as yet, with a few notable exceptions, there are great tracts of life that are not entered, and are hardly known of, by these existing agencies. There must be some influence which shall enter in and take possession of these tracts of life in the name of what is true and pure. The lines along which this influence shall act are varied, intricate, and ill-defined. It must come close to the lives of the people themselves. It must be keen and sensitive to every sort of delicate, subtle feeling they have. It must, in short, be a personal influence. The person must act in a close, continued intimacy with those to whom he comes; that is, he must be

a neighbor. He must join freely in the neighborhood life. He must have so varied an interest in
human affairs that he shall be able to enter actively
into sympathy on some side of life with every one
of them. He must not establish a propaganda.
He must not at first even have methods. He must
not set about building up one more institution.
He must not hurry. Above all, he must not be
anxious about results. The children of this generation seek for a sign, but there shall be no sign
given them; he must be content that the generations of the future shall see his work in its true
light. This person, therefore, must have the historic sense and the philosophic breadth of view.
He must love men, but deeper than all he must
love humanity. All these things mean that this
person must have drunk at the fountains of knowledge. One can hardly imagine an uneducated
person coming as a true prophet to that vast region
of life which is not mapped out, divided into
departments, called by names, and embraced within
a cultus. In the sociological pantheon this worship is at the altar of the Unknown God. The
worshipper must come not only with the zeal for
service, but with that eager, inquiring mind
through which he shall be led into varied and
constantly developing knowledge and power.

Now if we are bold enough to hold that civilization must do its work for the whole of society,
and for every class and every section of society,

we must, I think, see that it is absolutely essential
that such effort as has been indicated should be
undertaken, — not that it is interesting and com-
mendable that it should be undertaken, but that
if civilization is in any large degree to do its work
for humanity, such effort is essential. It is for
this reason that one dares to believe that the university settlements, small in number and slight in
results as yet, are destined to fill an important
place along with the many other forces which are
making for social progress. They come near to
fulfilling the conditions that have been laid down.
Their workers, like the people of the neighborhood, not only work there but live there. As college men and women, they have learned to a degree
how to live the good and beautiful life. As cultured persons, they believe in the saving quality
of every sort of influence which tends to make
men and women true to the human pattern. They
also take a scientific as well as a philanthropic
interest in learning accurately and comprehensively
just what the state of life is in their neighborhood.
They are able to compare this kind of life with
other kinds of life, and to see how each kind may
be bettered by taking up elements of the other
kinds. By their broader knowledge and sympathies, they are able to originate plans for bringing unused resources of society to meet its unfilled
needs, and are able to put into fuller operation
agencies that are already in one way or another
attempting to restore the balance.

A university, and a college in its measure, ought
to be the special exponent of advancing civilization. It stands not only for a knowledge of the
whole world as it is, but for the variety of human
interests and hopes. The troubles of society ought
to be most keenly felt there. That great masses
of men and women are cut off from the better life
of society, unknown and uncared for, is, rightly
considered, a direct imputation of shame upon
the university. It means that the cause of the
university is in danger. It means, also, that the
university is falling short of its full use. The university man or woman, that is, the truly cultured
man or woman, at the end of the nineteenth
century, is the one who ought to be able to go
everywhere through the world, filled with child- ·
like wonder, but never at the last capable of
being surprised. But, alas! how we find ourselves,
after our academical, and even after our professional courses, lost not merely in a vast body of
new facts, — that was to be expected, — but lost
in a maze of conflicting principles. There are
more things in life than are dreamed of in our
history, our political economy, or even in our
philosophy. The weak idealism with which most
graduates go into their life-work makes it inevitable that they should be racked and torn before
they have rightly estimated the forces of evil,
which must sometimes, in the narrower view of
things, seem to be the only forces there are. Cul-

ture has progressed by gradually imaging in itself all that goes to make up the world's life. But here are vast sections of mankind, whose life, for all that is distinctive of it, is practically an undiscovered country to those who most clearly stand for culture. How provincial our culture is. To how great a degree ignorant, to how great a degree selfish. How it generalizes about men, — the proper study of mankind is man, — and calls the result knowledge of them. How it satisfies itself with a distant echo of feeling for them. How often it develops effeminacy, instead of the strong, chastened refinement of the citizen of the world. Wrote Arnold Toynbee to his friends at Oxford: "Our delicate, impalpable sorrows; our keen, aching, darling emotions; how strange, almost unreal they seem by the side of the great mass of filthy misery that clogs the life of great cities."

The University Settlements, then, as the parent movement of University Extension, stand for a double sense of urgency on the part of the universities, — the necessity of giving what they have in abundance, and the necessity of gaining what they need in order to be true to themselves. There is a sort of sentimental cant which is indulged in by those who have but slightly touched the problem of the Settlements, which represents the university men and women as youthful martyrs bringing all that is illuminating into places of absolute darkness. "Elevation by contact" is a phrase which these like to use. There is also a cant of those who have seen somewhat more of Settlement work which represents the residents as combining together in a sort of club for the sake of a period of romantic existence which they in a measure justify by learning much out of the experience of their poorer neighbors. Let us clear our minds of cant. Let us, to begin with, simply remember that the university and the closely populated city quarter each need the other; and from that pass on to consider how the representatives of each can learn and do learn mutual helpfulness. But in judging the work of the Settlements one does not, I think, get the right point of view who looks at them apart from the great social changes which they in their measure represent. Looked at in the true perspective, one sees that the simple fact of a group of educated men or women taking up their residence in a poor part of a city is something of significance and value. The phrase "elevation by contact," ill-used as it has been, contains a truth in it. Let us not, in the endeavor to escape being patronizing, make the mistake of standing so erect as to lose our balance backward. The University Settlement comes into the district from without. It is, if you please, imposed upon the district. The residents come first of all to help, conscious of bringing with them resources that will be positive contributions to the life of the district. They should have no fond hope of galvanizing a higher existence into the people, making it seem, by a sort of *deus ex machina* illusion, as if the people had accomplished the result of themselves. They should continue to bring in from without the district a variety of helpful influences. They should abhor patronage as they abhor the curse; but they will soon learn that their poorer neighbors detect and despise false humility just as readily. The true attitude for every social worker is that of a member of a noble family, in which there is the widest inequality, but equality and inequality are never thought of, and greater knowledge and strength mean only greater love and service.

It is, of course, perfectly true that, novel as is the plan of the University Settlements, and considerable as is their value for bringing about and giving expression to the changed attitude of the educated classes to the working classes, yet their critical test will be whether they can justify themselves as establishments where men and women under organized direction shall become trained to do continuous, painstaking work of investigation and action, so that each Settlement shall be accomplishing the improvement of its own neighborhood, and shall, from time to time, send out skilled workers to continue similar efforts in other surroundings. This test, under a right understanding of what a University Settlement is in its motive and functions, every supporter of the Settlements will heartily welcome. The only caution that need now be made is that in the initial stages of the movement any strictures made upon it, in comparison with the work of established institutions or organizations following a few easily defined lines and acting through specialists of long experience, must be considered as resulting from a false estimate of what Settlement work is in idea, as well as of what, under its limitations, it must for some years yet be in fact. For the present, the work must be done by amateurs, for there are no professionals. It must not now and it may never be too closely organized, because it consists so largely of turning to social account delicate kinds of influence which cannot be borne through the channels of organization. And too much regularity and constancy must not yet be expected when those who enter this work have so largely to live upon locusts and wild honey, and to go clad in camel's hair.

The prime requisite in the minds of educated men in undertaking any task is to know to a greater or less degree the situation in which they are to work and the material which they are to work upon. The close, scientific study of the social conditions in the neighborhood about a Settlement is indispensable to its success. Of course, careful social analysis of a neighborhood demands the observation of months and years; but the task should be undertaken from the very beginning. The movement of the Settlements will be

false to its promise, it will cut off its own future,
if it do not know for itself, and tell thinking
people, and by its absolute statement of facts com-
pel thinking people to hear, how the other half
lives. The residents should become familiar with
all that goes to make up the life about them, —
what homes the people have, their sanitary condition, their privacy, their comfortableness, their
adornment; what food and drink the people have;
what clothes they wear; what work they do, and
all the questionable conditions that surround the
labor of men and women in these days; what wages
they receive, and how well or ill they spend their
money; what knowledge they are gaining; what
amusements they have; all the little amenities of
their lives; their cruelty, their unselfishness;
their loves, their hates, their sins, their crimes,
their hopes. Now this searching investigation can
never be made by the mere canvasser or statistician.
It comes only by long and loving acquaintance.
Science and sympathy must unite if we are to have
any living knowledge of the poor. This knowledge the University Settlements offer good promise
of giving, — after seeing the lives of the people
with that quickened vision which comes from a
warm heart, representing them again with the
faithfulness of the truth-loving mind. Such work
will, if it is seriously and systematically followed,
give to the residents a keen sense of what the
needs of the people are, in their just proportion

and relation, and will develop in them a selective
instinct for finding what may best be done to fill
their needs, and it will even make the situation
stand out before their minds until it shall induce
in them the thought of newer and better forms
of helpfulness.

After the study of the social statics of the neighborhood comes the study of its social dynamics.
What the people are accomplishing for themselves
both in their individual and home life, and in local
organizations for whatever purpose, is a matter of
absolute importance to a Settlement before launch-
ing into its more constructive activity.   Such effort
on the part of the people will indicate more truly
than anything else just where the greatest ground
for hope is.   The presumption is always against
having a Settlement introduce any new institutional
scheme.   It is always in favor of falling in with
the current of what is already advancing in the
neighborhood.   In an enterprise of the people's
own, you find them under a kind of momentum
which can never be so well artificially aroused.
Every original aspiration for better things becomes
to the resident of a true spirit something to be
known and understood, and then fostered with
tender care.   Every beginning of independent
organization has to him the interest that a rare
specimen has to a naturalist.   And so, gradually
by the united efforts of the residents, the Settlement, as a whole, comes to be in sympathetic touch

with the homes of its neighbors, and with all combined movements among them toward trade organization, co-operation, or thrift, or toward education
and recreation. And a Settlement is false to its
purpose if it do not take knowledge also of the
organized forces of sin that are at work in its
vicinity. Sometimes these are not to a great degree
developed out of the life of the neighborhood as
such, but are foisted upon it by persons of other
and more well-to-do neighborhoods. But even in
such a case, the neighborhood in question by no
means escapes the contagion of evil. The curse of
the poor is their poverty; often the sacred hearth-
stone of honest poverty must be within sound of
the revelry and debauchery of those to whom
society is pleased to give its greater rewards.
University Settlements must be courageous enough
and scientific enough to face the grim, inhuman
evils that flaunt themselves in what are termed
the less respectable sections of cities, the horror
of prostitution, the horror of drunkenness, and all
their accompaniments and consequences. The
time has come when the educated man and the
educated woman must no longer merely shudder
and turn away from the dark depths of life. The
educated person cares little for the words and the
ways of the sensationalist and the purveyor of artificial reforms. But he respects just as little that
form of refined selfishness which says, "These
things always have been and always will be; who
touches them touches pitch."

A Settlement must be intimately acquainted
with all other agencies which have come from
without the neighborhood, with the intention of
working for its improvement in some way or other.
From the broadest possible view of the means of
social progress, the residents ought to learn to
estimate how far these agencies do really upbuild
the people, and they ought to put themselves in
a position where they can intelligently acknowledge and under right circumstances join in the
good work that is being done. I think young
graduates entering into social work are in especial
danger of being too narrowly critical of the efforts
of sagacious people who have had a different sort
of training for life than they.   Their sense of proportion here often fails them.   It is of great importance to the whole movement of the Settlements
that other kinds of social workers shall not be
given cause to think of the residents as a group of
exquisites, who find value only in certain highly
refined methods, and condemn the rest because of
flaws they may find.   Often one's judgment as to
the value of certain kinds of work is greatly modified by fuller knowledge of the situation in which
the workers find themselves.   It is therefore the
business of the residents to give sympathetic study
to forms of work which are conducted with a lack
of taste and discernment, and even to those which
are undertaken from what may seem to be mistaken motives.   They must have the sense which

will enable them to see the value of the spirit of service under widely various forms. The *à priori* argument against any plan is almost worthless to the social investigator. What contribution does it make in its results to the living of life in this neighborhood, or in what way does it hinder the living of life in this neighborhood, are the questions for the men or women of a Settlement.

And so it ought to be a matter of deep interest to each resident to become thoroughly conversant with the neighborhood existence. He must have his conversation, his citizenship, there. From before the establishment of the Settlement through all its career, this process of acquaintance must continue. Who can say what vast results may come when a succession of educated men and women return to their more regular life in the home, in the business house, in the school and college, in the church, knowing from a living experience, through the daily use of all the senses, just what the life of the working classes, and the classes below them, actually is.

It is very important, for the first at least, that the Settlements should be located with a view to the most favorable opportunity for studying what is distinctive of the great metropolitan poor quarters. The first Settlements ought to be located where they can be within range of the variety of social problems which a city offers. There seems to be a current impression that a Settlement ought

to be placed in the very midst of the most degraded
and hopeless classes, and, when Settlements are
not so situated, it is not an uncommon experience
for some who have cherished mistaken sentiment
with regard to Settlement work almost to disparage
the purpose of those at work, as if they were seeking the crown without the cross. But the object
of a Settlement is distinctly to face the whole
problem of the less favored classes, and all the
different phases of it. The Settlement, therefore,
is best located where it can easily look every way,
— toward the very poor, toward the regularly employed working people, and toward the criminal
and vicious elements which are found in spots and
streaks in all degrees of outward respectability.
This is very important if the active work of the
Settlement for the improvement of the people is to
have the value of a comprehensive experiment. A
Settlement located in the midst of a slum could
deal with the people of the slum, but only as it
made over the slum by new buildings, could it
secure the interest of the better grades of working
people. The self-respecting poor are often as jeal-
ous of their social standing as a duchess of her place
in the order of precedence.

It is also an advantage for a Settlement to be
situated so as to be within easy reach of the whole
of the surrounding section of the city. In many of
our American cities there are already, or soon will
be, great metropolitan poor districts. In the midst

of these, rather than in distant and sequestered working-class quarters, the Settlement ought to be placed. Often there are other parts of the city that seem to be more needy, but they present a narrower range of problems, and are often so far away as to be practically separate villages or towns by themselves. Where the great forces of a city's common life are steadily developing a distinctively metropolitan poor district, even though the process has not advanced very far, there, both for the sake of the investigation and of the active work of social reform, is where the University Settlement ought to be, — if possible just out of hearing of the din and roar of traffic, and just out of sight of the glare of the evening promenade.

Of course, after the most casual preliminary investigation, the question begins at once to rise, What shall we do? And though there is danger in Settlement work of rushing too quickly into schemes for the improvement of the neighborhood, yet it is for the improvement of the neighborhood, above everything else, that the Settlement has come. And the first thing to do is to strengthen the things which remain. Every kind of centre of social life in the neighborhood should become the object of the wisest care that the Settlement can give. First of all, the Settlement should begin by being as nearly as possible a home. It is a disadvantage, I think, to have, from the first, easy public access to the house. The residents should be neighbors, and

should become acquainted in the same natural way
by which neighbors become acquainted in the simpler circles of society, — that is, they must neither
intrude, after the fashion of the census-taker, nor
must they hold coldly aloof until all the forms of
introduction have been gone through. The first
and constant effort of the Settlement should be to
have its men or its women come into relations of
friendliness and intimacy with the people in their
homes. The bringing out of the possibilities of
home life among the working people is one of the
most valuable results that a group of educated men
or women could aim at; and, of course, the women
residents can accomplish far more in this direction
than the men. It is a good plan to have one resident especially to visit in each of certain groups of
houses, such as can conveniently be classified; and
then, without hurry, or the use of mechanical means,
let him become thoroughly acquainted with the
people living there, with the purpose of bringing
the resources of the Settlement to bear upon that
quarter just as fully as the circumstances, when
they become known, will allow. As time goes on,
the homes of the neighborhood will be better in
their sanitary condition, in their food, in their reading, in their enjoyments, in their morals, and in
their religious life, through direction and assistance
from the Settlement. This department of the work
is capable of being systematically laid out and all
its needs provided for; and this kind of organiza-

tion might go on as rapidly as the residents could complete roughly the social analysis of the streets in which they undertake to visit.

Similar careful treatment must be given the local organizations. These will very rarely run on neighborhood lines, but the residents, in so far as they connect themselves with the organizations, ought to do so simply upon their claims as dwellers in the vicinity. It is even important that the residents should remain in the background so far as official position in such societies is concerned. In this way they can have a better influence, as they will remain outside of all the factional quarrels that rise out of the thirst for prominence. The Settlement ought to be represented, so far as possible, in every organization which has any visible influence in the local community, whether the object be one of vital interest or not, — the development of independent social forms is so important. As to the secret orders which are so common everywhere, it is a question whether it is worth while to take up at all with them. It certainly would not be well at the beginning to expend force in that way. But whatever trade unions, working-men's clubs, temperance societies, and even political clubs there are, ought to receive the sympathy, and so far as is possible without compromise, the active support of the Settlement. It is particularly important that the leaders of these organizations, and other influential persons of the neighborhood, should be made friends of, unless they are unworthy of friendship. It is perhaps needless to say that in all these relations the residents must be frank to recognize the ability and worth of the people whom they meet, acting naturally, whether as learners or teachers.

A work only second in importance to the encouraging of the inhabitants of the neighborhood in what they are doing for themselves is that of co-operating with all the good forces already active in the neighborhood which are not original developments of its own immediate life. In these would be included all the officers of the law, the teachers in the schools, the agents of charitable societies, and the clergymen in charge of the churches. In the case of aldermen and police officials, of course, the character of the men differs very widely. The policy of the Settlement ought to be, first, to make every possible effort to establish friendly relations with these men, and through such relations to secure a knowledge of the situation and increased effort for its improvement; but if these means fail, then the residents must use more forcible methods. There are many ways in which friendly acquaintance with the police can be of great use to a Settlement, especially if the residents are bound to know the whole state of their neighborhood. Moreover, there are few persons in the community more deserving of the sympathy and support of good people than an honest policeman located in a bad city quarter. He has to stem the tide of the city's moral defilement as no other person is called upon to do; and he is almost wholly deprived of the uplift, which nearly every social worker now feels, that comes from knowing of a great body of true men and women who are glad of the work he is doing. Another class of persons who make a valuable moral contribution to society and receive very little moral return at the hands of society is the school teachers. The residents of a Settlement can be of great use both in confirming them in what they already do well, and in assisting them to have better purposes and methods. The schools can be made in many ways better factors in the social development of the children than they now are, by the introduction of the many new methods of instruction, by the gradual addition of manual training to the curriculum, and by a larger use of school buildings for combined instruction and recreation.

The study and practice of scientific charity is a most important line of effort for a Settlement to undertake. Residents should join the local committees of such charities as are already organized; and while it is doubtful whether a Settlement should become identified with any charity to the extent of having its local headquarters in the Settlement house, yet certain members of the group ought to give themselves especially to becoming thoroughly acquainted with the state of the dependent and casual classes and to the skilful

administration of relief.   All organizations that
exist in the city for the care of children, for assisting in special ways the worthy but unfortunate
poor, for improving the dwellings of the people,
and for increasing facilities for public recreation,
should receive regular support, for the sake of
having their benefits brought more fully into the
neighborhood.

What shall be done with regard to co-operating
with the religious forces of the neighborhood?
On this question a variety of attitudes are taken.
Some say there is so much jealousy and partisan-
ship connected with religion that a Settlement
attempting to work on broad neighborhood lines
must be absolutely neutral on matters of religion.
Some others, admitting the difficulty, still say
that they will not remove from their programme
what they consider to be of so vital importance,
but will bring in that form of religion which they
think is the best, with the hope of gaining for it
the support of a part of those who are helped by
the other work of the Settlement.   I believe there
are very important reasons that both of these kinds
of Settlements should exist.   There are certainly
many city neighborhoods where an avowed religious connection would very much hamper the
work of the Settlement.   There are also many
men in these days, and some women, who can
work only with a non-religious Settlement.   On
the other hand, there are many who can work far

better under a definite religious standard. And
there are many places where a definite religious
allegiance is a help rather than a hindrance, — as
in the case of the Oxford House urging the claims
of the Church of England in Bethnal Green, and
the Scotch Settlements under strong Presbyterian
auspices in Edinburgh and Glasgow. There is a
third attitude which a Settlement may take, and
I think it is the most just of all. This position
is, that while a University Settlement, no more
than a university itself, should be committed to a
theological and ecclesiastical propaganda, yet both
must, if they are to have a mission to the whole
of men's higher life, be ready to meet men on the
religious side of their nature. From this point of
view, a Settlement ought to undertake its work
feeling the stirring of the religious motive. It
ought to be prepared to bring to the people the
influences of a broad and free religious enthusiasm,
which shall show the insignificance of differences
compared with the unity of spirit in which every
man is in some sense religious. So that while I
am free to admit very great practical difficulties,
I cannot feel that University Settlements are loyal
to their name if they suppress the influence of the
deep and broad religion which is to so large degree
current among the college men and women of
to-day — too full of sympathy and hope to stay
with scholastic dialectic, too sure that there is
but one religion to be unduly concerned as to the

varying forms it takes. From this point of view
it is an essential part of the residents' social work
in the neighborhood to enter into friendly co-operation with the religious work that is being done
there, especially with the hope of bringing in a
greater and greater element of that religion which
is pure and undefiled.

The part of the work of a University Settlement
which to the popular mind mainly gives it its
character is really least distinctive of it. The
establishment of new centres of social activity, the
development of new forms of institutional effort,
might possibly not demand residence in the neighborhood. But the work amongst the homes and
organizations of the people would be wellnigh
impossible to an outsider. Still, residents are at a
considerable advantage for the introduction of a
new program of means for social improvement,
especially if the foundation has been strongly laid
by making the Settlement first of all a hospitable
home, and by having the residents become welcome
guests in the homes of the people. But it cannot
be too forcibly stated that for a Settlement at once
to make an institution of itself is to lose nearly all
of the finer influence which it is the essence of a
Settlement to have. The motto of the University
Settlement movement is in the words of Mr. Barnett to the little group of pioneers at Oxford:
"Vain will be music, art, higher education, or
even the gospel, unless they come clothed in the

life of brother men." So much being said, the
possibilities in the way of the enlargement and
enrichment of life, such as may, in the course of
years and with the support of men and money, be
taken up by a Settlement, are so numerous and
varied that one can only touch upon them in
general outline here. As far as possible, these
lines of effort must be undertaken in the name of
the neighborhood, putting much responsibility upon
the people themselves for whatever may be attempted. The principle of self-help must be imparted to them at every turn. Only remember
that the people must be helped to help themselves.

The first and most obvious need of the life of
every poor neighborhood is healthful recreation.
The dulness and dreariness of its life is only the
reverse side of the brutality of it. Whatever is
done among the children and youth will centre in
boys' and girls' clubs, the success of which will
depend almost wholly upon the capacity of the
persons who have charge of them. There are no
proved and tried methods for carrying on a boys'
club. The girls' club is an easier matter. But
the person to lead a boys' club is born, not made.
In dealing with boys it is almost necessary to have
a gymnasium and drill hall where they can run off
their surplus spirits and be taught physical and
moral manhood at the same time. After that, the
hope of boys' clubs lies in manual training. It is
also practically settled that the big club of boys,

managed by one or two men as with long poles,
can never accomplish what needs being done.
There are also obvious difficulties about putting
into motion all the machinery of a club to meet
nightly for ten or fifteen boys. There is a compromise plan of having a large club with its nightly
meeting hall, which shall be divided into congenial
groups, each group to be under the special charge
of some friend, who shall hold group meetings, and
shall endeavor to keep up a close acquaintance
with the boys of the group. The problem of
arranging meetings for the women is again much
simpler than that of providing wholesome recreation for the men. In England, where the idea of
a working-men's club, either independent or patronized, is so well understood, the problem is much
simpler than in America. Our working-men have
hardly yet dreamed of organization for the sake of
general recreation and self-improvement; nor has
any one else gone far toward suggesting such a
thing to them. But whatever is done in these
ways, the Settlement should be a centre for social
gatherings which shall, from time to time, include
the different members of each family, bringing
men and women, boys and girls, together, that
they may learn of the grace and sweetness of life.

On the educational side, a Settlement may begin
with some of the simplest and most popular forms
of study, and from that even aspire to establish a
working-men's university; and as for lectures and

concerts and art exhibitions, it may gradually build
up a People's Palace. On the industrial side, it
can introduce experiments in the way of co-operative stores, co-operative industries, building and
loan associations, benefit and insurance organizations; it will bring working-men and university
men together, in order that they may learn from
each other about social questions; and it may, as
at Toynbee Hall they have several times successfully done, arrange conferences where capitalist,
working-man, and scholar may meet and review the
situation from their different points of view. On
the ethical side, it will try to bring to the people
the influence of the lives and teachings of the
world's great moral heroes. On the religious side,
— if it have an acknowledged religious side to its
work, — it will, in all wisdom, provide opportunities, for those who will, to advance in the better
life by refreshing the spirit of love from the springs
of faith and hope.

Thus far I have referred only to the duty of a
University Settlement to its own neighborhood;
and this its one great duty. But it has other
duties. It has duties to the general section of the
city in which it is placed, and to the city at large.
It has duties to the men or women who are its
residents and associated workers. It has duties
to the body of its supporters. And it owes it to
society at large to endeavor to secure the spread
of the principles for which it stands. For the

general district, the Settlement can mass its forces
of residents and sympathetic neighbors, and enter
into the movement for good citizenship, by urging
the support of worthy candidates for municipal
offices, by promoting measures for reform and improvement, and in general by organizing for action
as to public matters that closely affect the life of
the people.   The large social interests of the whole
district must be felt by the residents only less
keenly than they feel the claims of their own
immediate neighborhood, and any efforts which
promise to be of benefit to the district should find
the outspoken support of the Settlement.   There
will be some parts of the Settlement's regular work
in which it will be manifestly impossible and unde-
sirable to find a sufficient constituency in a single
neighborhood, so that to a degree there will be a
personal concern felt at the Settlement for many
families and homes outside of the immediate neighborhood.   In this way there will even be in the
relation of the Settlement to the broad district not
a little of that warmth of touch which it finds in
its relation to its nearer neighbors.

A University Settlement ought to be a stronghold
of that rising municipal loyalty which is in some
respects as noble as patriotism among the civic
virtues.   The method and trend of city government ought to be watched until it is thoroughly
known, and then patient and constant efforts made
to improve the type of officials, and the methods

of legislation and administration. Toynbee Hall now has its representative on the London County Council, and two representatives on the London School Board; and every Settlement ought to strive to follow this example. There are many cities now which are almost persuaded to make a beginning upon such a splendid program of social politics as London has undertaken; and the Settlements, by coming in with fresh knowledge of the subject, and without fear of being called socialist, may have a considerable share in the great results that are sure to come.

But a Settlement must represent a much larger notion of a city than that of the mere political aggregation. The city is one of the great nerve tracts of the social organism. It is glowing everywhere with a sustained community life. It is, therefore, the part of a Settlement to recognize and assist every united movement of the citizens which in any direction seems likely to make broader and truer the common life of the citizens; feeling sure that many of the lines of effort which are now thought to be philanthropists' dreams will, in due time, be seen to be public necessities.

The residents of a Settlement ought to be men or women of some kind of liberal training. The association of the Settlements with academical loyalties is meant to be inclusive, but not exclusive, — I have used the term " University Settlement " as being the original and generic one, hoping that

it might embrace all the similar forms of effort
which have taken their suggestion from the first
University Settlements. The objection made to the
term on the ground of patronage, is, I think, not
well founded. The colleges owe it to themselves
to remove the popular impression that they are
places where well-dressed and haughty young persons live and enjoy themselves for four years. In
any case, the specific name given to the individual
Settlement may be without any semblance of patronage. The residents should live without any
mark of asceticism about them, — especially not if
such things have to be artificially taken on. The
life of simplicity and frugality which includes the
usual necessities of civilized existence will be most
easily understood by the people who come to the
house. Parts of the house which are intended for
hospitable use may well have kinds of adornment
which the residents might consider too costly for
their own private satisfaction, wherever they might
be living.

As to the direction of the residents, there ought
to be just enough authority in the head worker to
make sure that unity and continuity are fairly kept
up in the work of the Settlement. It ought to be
possible at any time to turn the whole force of the
Settlement down a single channel. But in dealing
with the individual workers, I consider that it is
essential to the plan of having educated persons
doing intimate personal work, that the directions

of the head worker should wholly take the form of suggestions, except in some rare instances, when his command or veto should be subject to appeal to the body of residents or to the managing council. It is not well even that the personality of one person should overshadow the rest, unless that person have much greater experience than they. The general lines of action being assigned according to the inclinations of the residents, they ought to be expected to develop a great share of the invention and originality which their own field of effort demands. The head worker ought to know everything that is being done by all the residents, and ought to be ready to offer suggestions and cautions whenever they seem to be needed. His suggestions may be especially frequent and pointed if he find any residents who are inclined to turn Settlement work into a pastime. But, on the whole, it is indispensable to the scheme that every resident from the beginning should feel a possessive, creative interest in his own work; that he should feel not merely the cheerful glow of action, but that he should feel that lofty joy which the artist feels. Anything that hinders the entrance of such fine influence into the doing of the work will prevent it from being imparted as a result of the work. The life and soul of Settlement work is in the charm and magic which lingers about persons, with fetters off, and held only by a noble enthusi· asm.

Applicants for residence should be considered
both as to their fitness for social work and their
ability to work in harmony with the residents.
So far as possible, residents should give their
whole working time. In order to make sure of
this, each Settlement ought to be so financed that
scholarships should be provided for residents, and
it is a great advantage if they can pursue their
study and work under some academical connection.
In such ways, the casual, *dilettante* element can
gradually be removed out of Settlement work without in the least removing its appeal to the imagination. The head worker should be on an allowance sufficient to justify his giving a term of years
to Settlement work. It is, of course, well and
admirable for those who have means to live at
the Settlements at their own charges, but that is at
best an exceptional and temporary arrangement,
in this country at least.

The Settlements will have two classes of supporters : those at the institutions of learning, and
those living in and about the city where the Settlement is located. These supporters should be
organized into a body giving not only financial
support but moral support. Those who have the
true Settlement spirit do not come as envoys but
as forerunners. The colleges ought to be often
visited. Visitors ought to come often from the
colleges. The reports of the work and the results
of investigation ought to be regularly published.

The local constituency ought to be reached through a sort of extension bureau, which shall send out lecturers, organize reading clubs, and encourage and assist persons to begin active social work in their own neighborhoods. The Settlement ought to be to them a centre of inspiration and instruction, not as to the delegating of their duty, but as to doing it themselves. Thus also a body of associate workers will be in training, who will come regularly to the Settlement to take some part in its work, so as to relieve the residents of a large share of the more formal work, and leave them free for investigation, personal intercourse, and original experiment.

So much for the diagnosis; what of the prognosis? What can the Settlements accomplish, what future development is the idea likely to have, and what is it worth to society as a whole? University Settlements are capable of bringing to the depressed sections of society its healing and saving influences, for the lack of which those sections are to so large an extent as good as dead. The Settlements are able to take neighborhoods in cities, and by patience bring back to them much of the healthy village life, so that the people shall again know and care for each other. They will impart a softer touch to what social powers now act there; and they will bring streams from the higher sources of civilization to refresh and arouse the people so that they shall no more go back to the narrowness and gloom, and perhaps the brutality of their old existence.

The expansion of the Settlement method will come partly by its being taken up in greater or less degree by churches and charitable institutions and societies; but its greatest expansion will be through the increase of the Settlements themselves. These results will come as the body of trained Settlement workers gradually enlarges. There ought to be, and not impossibly will be, a University Settlement in each considerable neighborhood of every great city, and I do not make too bold when I say that there ought to be two in each neighborhood, one of men, and one of women. Then each neighborhood, made keen and vital with the social energy that has been stirred within it, would awake to the electric touch coming from every other neighborhood charged with the influences of social life, and would eagerly respond to each effort to ennoble the life of the city, until we should have whole cities tending to become what communities of men and women should be, places where the things that are pure and lovely and of good report shall become, by toil and suffering, the common inheritance, whose homes shall never be ignorant of what peace and love are; where even the streets should begin to tempt and fascinate boys and girls into the ways of righteousness, instead of luring them into the haunts of sin.

As a definite contribution to the agencies of social progress, the Settlements stand for the fact that there is no short and easy road to a better society, and that for every social gain there must be some corresponding expenditure of personal effort. They also show not only that social work demands a far greater number and variety of workers than has before been understood to be necessary, but that it demands the best type of men and women acting under the highest motives they can feel. Thus the Settlement movement strikes at the root of the tree. Not contrivances, but persons, must save society. And wheresoever society at all needs saving, there persons must go in ample number and of the best trained ability. The resources of society are largely in persons. The needs of society are in persons, and there must be overturnings and overturnings, till everywhere the resourceful shall be filling the wants of the needy.

The University Settlements are a message of life and hope to that increasing body of men and women in these days who are stifled and crushed under the gifts of society become impediments through disuse. The Settlements offer, as has never before been offered, an opportunity for the employment of every sort of faculty and attainment, so that every kind of person may begin to have to some degree the joy and enlargement of life that comes from a consciousness of power to make other life more

true to itself.   How the whole of human existence
becomes ennobled, when men and women begin to
understand that everything they know, and everything they are, is an image to them of what may
be modelled in the yielding clay of the lives of
others.

And this suggests how much the movement of
the Settlements may mean in the future to the colleges and universities, by showing them that everything which makes life better at the favored centres
will add to life at the far-out extremities; that
every element of culture is a means of grace; and
that all that makes up civilization will be quickened
at its source by giving it the broad amplitude of
humanity.   As a result of such influences, now
rising so fast, we shall find education taking anew
the larger measure of the world, and developing in
itself an impulse which will make its votaries no
longer merely priests at the altar, but apostles to
the world of men.   And so we may expect to see
the young men and young women of the future
come out from our colleges and universities trained
in a social sense, corresponding to the growing
intenseness of social relations, having perhaps not
more varied powers and attainments than the graduates of the present, but whatever sort of gift
they possess having with it a zeal for ennobling it
and themselves by using the gift in the service of
men that do not have it.   The University Settlement will then become an organic part of the uni-

versity, one of its professional schools perhaps,[1] where every sort of latent or narrowly applied power which the university develops shall be strongly called out, and sent along lines where it shall begin to be applied to its appropriate function of ministering to the common life of society.

The University Settlements stand for a sublime faith in everything that goes to make up the good and beautiful life. I wonder if since the Renaissance there has been any such assertion of the life-giving quality of culture as our simple Settlements stand for, — pledged to a belief in its message and mission to all sorts and conditions of men, gradu-

---

[1] The necessity of dealing with the life of the masses of the people, which makes hospital and dispensary work so important to the medical student, is now being felt in a marked degree at the theological seminaries. For several reasons the work of a Settlement of theological students must be nearly identical with that of a general University Settlement; the only difference being that the religious motive will always be kept prominent, and methods of religious work will receive more particular attention on the part of the residents. But the same comprehensive program must be followed. The belief in the helpful influence of every good thing must still be held. Nearly as great a variety of workers can be, and ought to be, called into service. The vast majority of the people in the depressed sections of cities who are inaccessible to direct religious effort are as distinctly a part of the constituency of one sort of Settlement as of the other; and they must be appealed to upon such sides of their better nature as are sensitive to appeals. Every Settlement must go patiently to work with the hope of developing means for saving the whole of its neighborhood; for making all the people who dwell in the neighborhood regenerated in every part of their lives.

ally demonstrating that the things which go to
make up culture are, in the broadest and deepest
sense, humanities.

It may seem to some in a high degree over-con-
fident to trace out of this small movement of the
Settlements an influence toward so great results.
There is one thing that University Settlements have
contributed to the life of the present which cannot
be gainsaid. They have made work among the
poor interesting, which before seemed dull and
wearisome. They have shown opportunities for
intelligent men and women in such work that were
unknown before. They have cast about social service the glamour of the moral picturesque. Whenever such an accomplishment is made, through a
great genius or under some common inspiration of
a group of men, the hand on the dial of human
progress perceptibly moves forward. For the task
of the future is to learn to see in human life the
attraction which we now are able to see in nature;
and to work out for humanity the beauty and the
glory which the world about us prefigures and pre-
dicts. And so we shall go further than to see the
spirit of God brooding upon the face of the waters,
to feel that the hills are filled with his legions, to
find every bush a burning bush and every rock an
altar; for we dare to hope for the time when man
shall begin everywhere to visit man, his brother,
and every visitor shall be a wrestling angel, joining
with his brother in loving emulation of what is

strong and true, making him to know the weakness
of the lower life, showing in himself, all uncon-
sciously, a vision of the better life, giving the man
a new name to express the promise of the future,
and leaving him with a heavenly benediction.

IV.

PHILANTHROPY — ITS SUCCESS AND FAILURE.

By James O. S. Huntington, Order of the Holy Cross,
Westminster, Md.

From the first founding of the New England colonies up to the beginning of the present century philanthropy in this country was in its merely rudimentary and inchoate condition. No trace is to be found in the annals of that period of many of our most familiar and successful charities. There were no Fresh Air Funds, no St. Andrew's Coffee-stands, no Day Nurseries, no Newsboys' Lodging Houses. The principal charitable institution was one in the neighborhood of Boston, for the instruction of Indian lads. It was called "Harvard College." Family traditions and the anecdotes related by our grandfathers and grandmothers make us familiar with the social life of those early days. Comforts were few and work was hard; many of the very necessaries of to-day were unknown; but the problems of pauperism and mendicancy had not presented themselves. There were plenty of kindly acts done for those under one or another form of temporary difficulty or need, but they could hardly be dignified with the name of philanthropy. They were nothing but the friendly deeds of neighbors, done as a matter of course, and regarded as entitling the doer to no special credit here or hereafter; in many cases they were *mutual* benefactions, and the recipient of the favor this year returned it the next. What poor people there were, — old folks who had come into the community late in life and had no one specially related to them, weak-minded and imbecile persons, chronic invalids, — were provided for at the "poorhouse," generally a farm on public land under the care of some good-natured man and his wife who looked upon their charges simply as unfortunate human beings, not as scientific cases. But, indeed, the whole community held itself more or less responsible for its dependent members, and if the inmates of the poor-house, wearying of its monotony and confinement, chose occasionally in pleasant weather to wander round a while from farm to farm they were usually tolerated and a place found for them at the table, perhaps even a bed in the attic, or a shake-down in the barn. To be sure, under such a system, or rather want of system, there was a possibility of individuals taking advantage of the open-hearted hospitality, and shifting along without doing much for their own support; but public opinion is a mighty force even in a thinly-settled country, and where everybody was

expected to work if he could, and almost every
one was busy building up or maintaining a homestead, it required a good deal of independence and
of originality, — or of natural "cussedness," — to
do nothing. Probably in most villages there were
two or three people who fulfilled these conditions;
they are the "Sam Lawsons" and "Jerry Lanes"
of New England romance; but they were endured
with a philosophic fortitude, partly, no doubt,
from a feeling that they furnished a sort of foil
to the general energy, and served some good purpose in retarding the too feverish activity of society
at large.

But in the third and fourth decades of this century a change began to make itself felt, at first, of
course, in the cities, but extending outward in
wider and wider circles, and increasing with ever
accelerating speed. The old homogeneity of society was broken up, and a pauper class began to
make its appearance. In the 'forties we note the
rise of the tenement-house system, in New York,
and similar conditions of dirt and over-crowding
in Boston and other places.

The "new occasions" brought "new duties,"
and philanthropy advanced to meet them. The
City Mission of the Episcopal Church in New York
was organized in the year 1831, the New York
Association for Improving the Condition of the
Poor in 1843; and about this time in Boston, Dr.
Tuckerman set on foot certain efforts, afterwards

known as the " ministry at large," which struggled bravely to stem the tide of pauperism in that city.

These and other societies undertook to direct the efforts of charitably-disposed individuals in seeking to relieve the miseries of the emigrants who were coming, — from Ireland at first as from other European countries later on, — to swell the ranks of poverty already rising on our own soil. It may be asked, " Why was not State aid forth-coming, sufficient to meet the wants of these people, without the intervention of private beneficence ? " That is a natural question. It might seem as though it would be a great saving of time and labor on the part of individuals to hand over the whole matter of relieving the necessities of people to the proper officers who either by " outdoor " relief (aiding families with doles of money or goods in their own homes) or by " indoor " relief (support of individuals in alms-houses, hospitals, orphanages, etc.), might prevent actual starvation and assist the worthy for a time or permanently as should be necessary. But a long and bitter experi-ence in England had put this country on its guard. The ruinous effect of the old Poor Law in England, under which the income of everybody, the strong as well as the weak, was supplemented up to a fixed standard out of the " rates," had proved that a great deal of suffering and distress must be left to be met from the voluntary gifts of private charity.

The moment it is understood by the idle and shift-less in a community, such as we find in one of our modern cities, that they can, on the ground of des-titution, claim a certain amount of support while still remaining at large and enjoying the sweets of liberty, the door is opened to a perfect flood of pauperism and consequent vice. Not only that, but a premium is at once put upon laziness, and the wages of self-respecting workers are dragged down by the competition of those who are eking out their earnings by receiving public support. Whether this is not true in large measure of *private* relief, we shall have occasion to consider by and by; the point to notice now is that it affords entire justification for the State refusing to attempt to cover the whole field of charitable relief, and abandoning, as it is doing more and more, any attempt to distribute outdoor doles.

Before leaving this subject, however, as not im-mediately before us in the study of philanthropy (*i.e.* voluntary beneficence), I would quote one pregnant sentence from Dr. Thomas Chalmers be-fore a Parliamentary Committee on the Poor Law for Ireland : —

" I think it is one evil of public charity that the poor, who are not very accurate arithmeticians, are apt to overrate the power of a public charity, so that the real relaxation of their habits, not being proportional to the amount given, but being pro-portional to the amount expected, leaves them

in greater misery than if no such public charity
were instituted."

While there had always been a prejudice, more
or less strong, against state aid for the poor, it was
supposed that aid given by voluntary benevolent
societies would not pauperize because it could not
be claimed as a right. But, in spite of hopeful
expectations, evils very soon presented themselves.
The existence of a number of different centres of
relief created the temptation to make a living by
becoming a beneficiary of all of them. Door-to-
door begging was already in vogue; but the societies offered much wider scope for the peculiar
arts and the ready ingenuity of the "rounder."
Thus a class of professional mendicants appeared,
as far superior to the old-fashioned beggar as
the expert "boodler" surpasses the common
sneak-thief. Lists of the patrons of charitable institutions, even lists of pew-owners at fashionable
churches, passed into the hands of men who had
decided that the world owed them a living, and
who proposed to take it with as little trouble to
themselves as possible. There followed a stream
of letters written by people in apparent distress,
ranging from the note on delicately scented
paper, from a lady who had suddenly met with a
calamity that left her penniless among strangers,
but who would certainly receive a remittance next
week, to the blind negro clergyman who sent
round a dirty subscription paper asking for a con-

tribution to enable him to join his wife and children in Savannah, and the man who was anxious to buy himself a wooden leg, — though if the leg had represented the money collected for the purpose, it would have been, like the famous Miss Kilmansegg's, of gold rather than wood.

These letters were supplemented by visits from people who asked for money under every imaginable pretext, and with varying measures of success. Then there were bogus societies for all kinds of purposes, and the very methods that genuine philanthropy had devised for raising funds were copied by those who sought to divert the gifts of tender-hearted people into their own pockets. The streets began to be infested with a long succession of impecunious persons, in every variety of seediness of attire, down to the half-clad gamin and the man with coat buttoned up to his chin, redolent of alcohol but equally guiltless of shirt and soap. Perhaps those to suffer most were the churches. Expert solicitors for alms seemed to take a peculiar delight in "doing the pious." They generally presented themselves in the *rôle* of converts, entirely indifferent as to their temporal concerns, but fully convinced of the faith of the congregation they wished to join. They could usually count upon enough sectarian jealousy and denominational rivalry to make their pretences go down. It became clear that something was needed to cope with this rank growth of importunity and deceit which threatened to exhaust all the vitality of true philanthropy. In the year 1877, the Charity Organization Society of Buffalo was formed, the pioneer of many societies of the same general character. The object of these associations was to bring the various relief agencies into mutually helpful relations with each other and with the department of the public relief, the police force, the work-house and the schools, and so enable all the different institutions to act harmoniously together for the repression of fraud, the adequate provision for the wants of those really deserving help, the reclaiming of those pauperized by the mistakes of the past, the encouragement by various schemes of thrift and self-help, and the removing of social abuses. This was a large program, and it involved for its carrying out the co-operation of many persons disposed to regard each other with more or less suspicion. But, notwithstanding the many difficulties to be overcome, Charity Organization Societies have been established in seventy-three of the cities and towns in the land. These are all in communication with each other and with like agencies abroad. It has not proved possible to bring *all* the many charities in the larger cities into the movement, but enough have joined to make the plan very effectual in the prevention of " overlapping " and the hunting down of impostors and suspects. The New York Charity Organization Society has a card catalogue, containing a record of a hundred and sixty thousand cases. As these reports are open for reference, by any duly accredited philanthropist, and by all the other seventy-three kindred societies from Maine to California, it may be seen that a very extensive machine has been created for the purpose of blocking the way of the man or woman who tries to live by mendicity and mendacity. Whether the engine sometimes strikes wildly, and hits the wrong man and maims for life, is a further question that does not concern us now. It is a question that will be likely to interest according as one belongs to the class that investigates or the class that is investigated.

While much of the work of the Charity Organization Society is of a detective character, it has also established a penny savings-bank system, conducted with much business ability. There are now 20,901 depositors and $10,644.79 deposited. The patrons of the bank are not limited to New York City, but are found as far away as Pittsburgh, Pennsylvania.

Most of the earlier societies had for their chief purpose the relief of bodily maladies and physical necessities. The schools, indeed, were teaching or trying to teach the children the rudiments of knowledge, the three R's at any rate, and a smattering of other things; but the schools hardly come under the head of philanthropic institutions. With our public-school system they are wanting in the voluntary character essential to philanthropy as we understand it. The churches, too, were instructing grown-up people and children in the dogmas of religion, and, in some measure, in the principles of morality; but this, again, lies beyond the compass of philanthropy in the conventional sense. So that, for the most part, the charitable societies regarded people as receptacles for food and as requiring clothes, shelter from the cold, and, in sickness, doctors, nurses, and medicine.

Gradually, however, a truer conception of human nature asserted itself, and provision was made for other than animal wants. Instruction of children in the Kindergarten system of Froebel began to do a gracious work in quickening the perceptions and opening the eyes of the children of the poor. So fully have its uses been proved, that it seems a disgrace that the State should still leave its infants to be taught by private beneficence. In St. Louis there are over six thousand little children in the eighty-five public Kindergartens as part of the common-school system. The New York Board of Education has just determined to introduce Kindergartening in the Primary Schools of that city. Industrial training follows naturally upon the Kindergarten. This, too, is still left in many places to the care of volunteer philanthropy, though in Philadelphia and Chicago it plays an important part in the regular curriculum of the schools. To New York belongs the credit of having origi-

nated the method of kitchen-gardening that has
done so much to give back to household work its
dignity as one of the fine arts. When I was going
about among the tenement houses on the East Side
of New York, I could often tell on entering a
room that the children had been to the Wilson Mission by the neatness and brightness that reigned
there. A step beyond the cooking class, the sewing school, and the whittling class, takes us to
the trade schools. The value of these in giving
to young men a wider knowledge of the principles
of their trade, than they could ever gain in a mere
apprenticeship, is not acknowledged as generally
as it should be. Especially among wage-workers
there exists the most unfortunate and childish
prejudice against them. That they do not accomplish all that their founders hoped for we shall
notice in due time.

In the elaboration of this system of industrial
training, philanthropy had made a distinct advance in recognizing its subjects as not only consumers but at least potential producers as well.
But other powers and capacities in human nature
called for recognition. Man eats and works ; so
does the ox. But man is created also to enjoy,
and his capacities for enjoyment put him into
communication with fields of being of which the
mere animal cannot faintly dream. Some of those
whose thought and care were given to the poor
felt that their work was hardly begun until they

could waken into activity those distinctly human faculties of social intercourse, of intellectual pleasure and artistic delight, which for themselves made the world so fair and life so well worth living. It would seem as though this were a proper function of the State-supported school system; but it will probably take several generations yet to convince taxpayers that it is not a waste of money to teach the rising generation how to be simply and rationally happy. On the London School Board a few men and women fought for months to secure the introduction of pianos into the Board schools. They have now been withdrawn. But voluntary effort is not hampered by the timidity of salaried officials and the necessity of suiting oneself to party politics. And an enlightened philanthropy is now moving forward on to the new ground of bringing to the people the best there is in social pleasure, in literature and music, and science and art. This subject has already been treated in this volume. It is, therefore, unnecessary for me to dwell upon it.

I would, however, add one incident as illustrating the eagerness the poor will manifest for what is really beautiful. The Apollo Club in Chicago numbers, among its four hundred members, some of the wealthiest people in the city. A few winters ago the leader, Mr. Tomlins, was conducting a rehearsal, and was just in the midst of a chorus that required his unswerving attention, when a

messenger-boy came in with a telegram. Mr. Tomlins left him waiting until the chorus was finished;
then he stepped down and begged the boy's pardon
as though he had been a young prince, and ex-
plained the reason for the delay. As he took the
telegram he happened to look in the lad's face; to
his surprise he saw that he was deadly pale, his
mouth was agape, and the tears were streaming
from his eyes. As soon as the boy could get his
breath he exclaimed, " Oh, sir, I wish you'd waited
two hours, I never heard anything like it in my
life."

Mr. Tomlins said nothing at the time but after
the rehearsal he remarked to a friend, " If there's
that kind of hunger in the people we shall have
to feed them."

So some weeks later, before the club broke up
for the summer, Mr. Tomlins said to the members,
" I want to remind you that you can never rise
to the height of Art unless you use it for the
highest purposes, unless you use it for the People.
You are intending to give four oratorios next winter in the new Auditorium; you will sell season
tickets at from five to seven dollars a seat. What
I propose to you is that you repeat every performance the next night for wage-workers and sell the
tickets at fifteen and twenty-five cents." " They
wouldn't care to come," somebody said. " Try
them," was Mr. Tomlins's answer.

When the Apollo Club met in the autumn it

was decided that the suggestion of the leader
should be carried out. The first oratorio to be
given was " The Messiah." Arrangements were
made to repeat it the next night with exactly the
same care, not an instrument less. To make sure
that the tickets reached the wage-workers they
were sold at the factories. The Auditorium holds
forty-five hundred people. There was a demand
for twenty thousand tickets. I reached Chicago
the following morning. A friend met me at the
train. We had hardly greeted each other before
he began to tell me about the oratorio. "I have
heard the Hallelujah Chorus twenty-five times," he
said. "I always knew there was something in it
that I had never heard, — but I heard it last night."

The plan of College Settlements and University
Extension is spoken of as derived from England;
but it is pleasant to remember that before Frederick
Dennison Maurice and his friends established the
Working Men's College in London, the forerunner
of Toynbee Hall and Oxford House, the principle
of enlisting wage-workers in the pursuit of literature and science had already found expression in
this country, and the factory-girls on the Merrimac
were bringing out the " Lowell Offering," and in
the Essex Institute in Salem mechanics and mar-
iners were making contributions to Botany and
Geology.

University Extension in East London and Hull
House in Chicago bring us up to date. They seem

to be the last venture of philanthropy, though so
unlike many of the efforts that have borne that
name that one does not wonder at their disown-
ing it.

This hurried sketch of the development of charitable work among us may afford a clue to the
conditions that are essential to success in philanthropy, to such a success as will make philanthropy a factor in social progress. Let us then,
in the light of the experience gathered in these
past failures and achievements, look a little more
closely into the real nature of our subject.

Philanthropy finds its origin in sympathy or
fellow-feeling for one's kind. This, as a mere
impulse, is not found only among men. It may
be traced also among the higher animals. Wolves
fall upon a wounded comrade and devour him.
Many domestic animals, on the contrary, show a
real pity towards one another. A well-fed dog has
been known to dig up a bone he had buried and
give it to a half-starved cur. We all remember
the story of the dog, whose leg had been bound up
by a kind stranger, bringing another dog to be
treated. But such actions are not regarded as
necessary to the nature of a brute. On the other
hand sympathy for one's fellows is by us regarded
as *proper* to man as man. To refuse it is looked
upon as *inhuman*. We reckon it as a " dictate of
humanity " to pity the wretched and to provide
for the starving and homeless. Each of us would

instinctively turn out of our way to help a man in sudden illness or distress.

But there are two ways in which such actions may be instinctive in any particular person. First, they may be instinctive in man much as they are in the brute. Here there is no reflection upon the act, it has no moral content, inasmuch as it involves no conscious movement of the will. Perhaps if the person were to stop and think about the kindness he is moved to do to his neighbor, to become conscious of himself as on the point of doing it, he would leave the deed undone. He might even feel ashamed at himself for having thought of doing it. He may have set up for a misanthrope, and despise himself for having been betrayed into something for which his philosophy furnishes no justification. Or, on the other hand, the person may be living in such simple and right relations with the world, that to act kindly and justly towards those round him, seems inevitable. He does not dream of doing otherwise. This is the first way in which philanthropic actions may be instinctive.

But, secondly, such actions may be instinctive as the result of long discipline and self-mastery, the outcome of habits established only after many a weary battle with selfishness, of correspondence with human relations when all the impulses of the lower nature urged one to thrust them aside. Now, as in the individual, so in society, both sorts of "instinctive" benevolence may be found. There is, first, the time of simple and primitive conditions; after that, the period of struggle with temptation; to a hard and unfeeling egotism, *then*, if humanity is victorious in the battle, the better day of proved virtue and self-determination towards the good, which has been seen with ever clearer vision as self-interest was subordinated to truth and principle was preferred to pleasure.

But the working out on to this higher ground demands a transformation of the unconscious or only half-conscious fellow-feeling by the infusion of a true rationality. It becomes a sacred duty, therefore, not alone to do the right but to know it as right, because it is the expression of the true. In this lies the sole path to a real freedom. "Ye shall know the truth and the truth shall make you free." Philanthropy succeeds just so far as it consciously seeks to know the truth as to the vital and necessary relations of men to each other in society and to act fearlessly upon them. If there is failure it is because these relations are being forgotten or wilfully ignored.

Let us look back over the road we have travelled and test this principle. In the healthful conditions of our early Settlements we easily recognize the period of unconscious and infantile good-will. In those days nothing seemed more natural than to accord to any one, friend or stranger, the temporary help asked for, food and drink, fire-wood, seed-corn, the loan of tools, etc. But when this same thing is done in a city like New York under entirely different social conditions, the act proves to be disastrous in its results. Then it becomes necessary to pass from a mere unthinking benevolence, and use the reason to consider in what relation one stands to the unfortunate man or woman before one, and in what way, and by what course of conduct, one can correspond to that relation.

This requires effort, it requires time, it requires probably looking into dirty places and meeting dirty people. At once a conflict ensues. Selfishness says, " Don't waste your time over the fellow; give him a nickel and let him go." Conscience pleads, " Something is amiss here; this man ought not to be in such a strait that he must go about begging, and in such a moral poverty that you cannot give him the help he asks without making him poorer still. This man is your fellow; you must find out the cause of his unhappy condition, and try and reinstate him in his manhood again."

These counsels are mutually exclusive; they imply two quite contrary views of the beggar before you. According to the first you owe him nothing but a contemptuous dole given to be rid of him or as an act of conventional decency, given, perhaps, with no more of pity for him than actuates saloon-passengers on an ocean-steamer when they throw sixpences on to the lower deck to see the emigrants or the stokers scramble for them. Very possibly the beggar may be much more ready that you should treat him in this fashion than that you should be guided by the light of conscience. He may be as selfish as you are, and as ready to ignore any real and personal relation between himself and you. He may regard you as a giver of sixpences just as you regard him as a receiver of them. Possibly that seems to you a very satisfactory arrangement on both sides. It would be if it were true, but it is damnably false. And, being false, it blinds and darkens and confuses more and more, and begets other falsehoods which blind and darken and confuse in their turn. But falsehoods do not last, days of judgment or discrimination, " crises " (separations) we call them in historical language, arrive, and then you have to deal with men who suddenly see what they have lost through the lie by which you have profited, and you have Paris in July, 1789, or Homestead in July, 1892. Revelation has led to revolution.

But suppose we acknowledge the claims of conscience. Then we set to work to find out how we can really help the man. But we are not out of the woods yet. We have recognized that *some* relation exists between him and us; but is it a *human* relation? " Case 15,237 " has not a very human sound. A man does not call his wife a " case," at least it is not regarded as a complimentary term. We may recognize a man as a man, only with a qualification attached; as a member of the *genus*, for example, though of a different *species* from ourselves. And we cannot too constantly remember that our conduct towards him will be determined exactly by the view we take of him.

No doubt we shall find a certain pleasure in looking on him as a subject for our scientific examination, our condescending patronage, our philanthropic investigation. I believe we can all plead guilty to having yielded to that temptation. I certainly do. Let no one think that I wish to condemn others while sparing myself. If I shall seem to criticise the methods of charity organization, I do not wish to conceal the fact that I was one of three to establish in the year 1878 the Bureau of Labor and Charities in Syracuse, the eighth society of the kind in this country. And in what I have said in the earlier portion of this paper, I have pointed out with some distinctness, I think, the imperative need that existed for something to accomplish the results aimed at by the movement of charity organization.

What I ask now is whether the system has not failed of its highest object, " To procure work for poor persons who are capable of being wholly or partially self-supporting," and " To promote the general welfare of the poor by social and sanitary reforms, and by the inculcation of habits of providence and self-dependence." No doubt there are some supporters of charity organization who will resent even the raising of such a question. But I desire to quote for their benefit the following passage from the address of the President of the New

York Charity Organization Society at the annual
meeting in the year 1888 : —

" I have attended meetings of this Society when
almost every speaker raised a laugh by some
amusing anecdote of detected imposture. I have
joined in the laugh as heartily as any one, but
I left such meetings with a sense of painful disappointment. I have craved some more positive
good. Do not understand me as underestimating
the importance of detecting and punishing fraud,
but I think I voice the sense of our members, in
looking back over last year's work, when I say
that we dwell rather on the 558 families made
self-supporting than on the 415 frauds exposed;
and when it comes to the beggars, not one per
cent of whom were deserving, I am more proud
of the 278 who were persuaded to desist without
arrest than of the 87 hardened cases who were
convicted and punished. One of our older members, who has a habit of speaking his mind, once
said that, our society was on sure ground until
it found a worthy case, and then it was all at
sea."

Of course, it is not to be forgotten that the
Charity Organization Society does not exist for
the purpose of giving aid or distributing alms.
But it does intend to benefit the needy, not merely
to save the pockets of the rich. And it is the
bringing together and organizing for more effective work of societies that exist simply for the

purpose of ministering in one way or another to the wants of the poor.

If those charities are doing useful work separately, there is no reason why they should not do better work in conjunction. If there be any radical mistake in the individual relief-agencies that vitiates their efforts, *that* will be likely to show itself only more plainly when they are organized. Or, to recur to the phraseology we have already used, if there be a lack of full recognition of the real and necessary relations that exist between men as men, whether poor or rich, on the part of the various constituents out of which the Associated Charities is formed, that association will not accomplish the task before it of "promoting the general welfare of the poor" unless it rises to a higher and truer conception and lifts up its component parts with it.

Philanthropy cannot be a factor in social progress unless it is itself progressive. Now, I do not think that we can deny that there is just such a lack of recognition of necessary relations, or at least of an out-spoken declaration of them, in that line of philanthropic endeavor that is summed up and centralized by the charity organization societies. In almost all these bodies the notion lurks that while we, the refined and respectable and well-to-do classes, have a kind of relation to the illiterate and the poor, — a relation that imposes duties of compassion and benevolence and charita-

ble offices, — yet that the relation is that of supe-
riors to inferiors, of higher to lower, of patrons to
clients.

"But," you will rejoin, "is not that the truth?
Can anything be plainer than that we are in a
more favorable position than these ignorant and
dirty people? Are we not possessed of powers
of mind and a breadth of knowledge, to say nothing of material wealth, that make us naturally
the guides and protectors of the poor? Is it not a
duty laid upon us, which we are striving to fulfil?
Are we not to consider ourselves as stewards of
our gifts and talents, and must we not seek
to use them wisely for our poorer brothers and
sisters?"

I am quite familiar with that language; with
shame I confess that I have used it myself; but I
declare that on the lips of most of us I believe it
to be rank with hypocrisy and hollow with deceit.
I do not say that we are all consciously hypocritical
or deceitful; but that when we talk in that fashion
we are using phrases that have been employed to
bolster up almost every tyranny and despotism
that has cursed Christendom in the last fifteen
hundred years. For what is really meant by these
complacent expressions? Do we in the least mean
that we regard the poor as people of the very same
stuff as ourselves, actually our brothers and sisters
under a common Father, who is too righteous and
loving to show favor or partiality, or to exempt

one set of His children from the healthful and life-giving rules which He lays upon the rest?

Do we mean that we have no right to expect of the poor anything that we are not willing to do ourselves, that we are not *trying* to do as faithfully as we can with the means at our disposal and consistently with the work for humanity that falls to our share? Do we mean that we never condemn in the poor anything that we do not as frankly condemn in ourselves and our acquaintances, and the members of our own favored class? Do we mean that we are always prompt to make allowances for the poor, and if they do not in all instances rise to the high level of virtue where we are so conscious of standing, ask ourselves whether we should have done any better if we had always lived in one room with six other people, learned to lie as soon as we could talk, and worked in a sweating-shop from ten to twenty hours a day ever since we were twelve years old? Do we mean this?

We mean nothing of the kind. What we do mean, — however we may gloss it over with glib phrases and hide it from our own eyes, — is that somehow, by some provision of nature or of God, we have been established on a distinctly different basis than that on which the poor stand, we are not under the *régime* that governs and must govern them, we are not of the same household. We belong to the House of Have; they belong to

the House of Want; and the rules of one family
are not the rules of the other.

This is not a statement that is popular with
most of us professional philanthropists, but it happens to be true, and it is of very immediate bearing
upon the question before us, how far philanthropy
is a factor in social progress. Not only that; it is
the question that is of practical concern. For we
live in a time when the eyes of wage-workers, of
the "poor," are being opened to the real worth of
our professions and the sincerity of our declarations
of affection for them. If we will not go forward to
accept the truth that is already making itself plain
to them, our so-called philanthropy will become
one of the barriers they must sweep away in the
process of their own emancipation and self-development. Let us, then, courageously examine this
question.

In the first place, it is one of the accepted principles, in all societies at all recognized by charity
organizations, that it is the duty of the poor to
work so far as they have strength and opportunity
to do so. Indeed, it is generally assumed, — no
tiresome investigation of the real state of things
being thought necessary, — that the opportunity
does exist, and that the able-bodied man or woman
could work if he had a mind to. At any rate, what is
taken as an axiom is, that any one convicted of
refusing work at *any* wages when he could do it,
is *ipso facto* beyond the pale of public or private

support, and, if he tries to support himself by mendicancy, is a fit subject for penal correction.

The Scripture passage usually quoted on the matter is 2 Thessalonians iii. 10, " if any would not work, neither should he eat." I entirely agree with this requirement; I hope, before I close, to give some evidence of how entirely I agree with it. But the point now to be noted is, that while the duty of working for a living is always emphasized when the poor are in question, the charitable societies with remarkable unanimity disregard, and thereby practically deny, the existence of any such duty on the part of the rich.

It is not merely that these societies do not go about in the fashionable quarters of the city inculcating this duty (although that might be as effectual a way of " promoting the welfare of the poor by social reforms " as trying to make people self-respecting by setting them to split wood by hand at fifty cents a day), but that a good many of the most prominent supporters of these societies are people who have never done a full day's work in their lives, and who consume in one week more than they could produce in a year at such unskilled labor as most of them are alone able to perform, and who not only do nothing themselves, but who withdraw from any useful occupation a still larger number of able-bodied parasites in the form of servants, flunkies, footmen, etc.

These are the people who largely maintain the

Employment Societies, the Refuges, the Orphan
Asylums, the Soup Kitchens and Soup Schools, the
Free Hospitals, the Flower Missions, etc.   They
are directors and trustees and patrons and patronesses and members of councils and advisory boards.
They form sewing-circles and sew for the poor, and
institute fairs and sales and raffles, and dispose of
useless things for exorbitant prices, and laugh and
joke and flirt for the poor, and finally get up a ball
and dance them in, destroying in the course of
their operations ten times as much as they event-
ually give to those in want.   And in recognition
of this heroic devotion to the interests of their unfortunate brothers and sisters, they are elected
as officers and managers of the Bureau of Associated Charities.

" But," it will be said, " you are entirely mistaken about the supporters of most of our charities; they are by no means idle people; they are
almost all of them men in the thick of business
life, who are working hard to support their families and leave something for their children."

That many such people give generously to
charitable societies, I do not for a moment question; but that a person such as I have described
would not be accepted as a donor, and compli-
mented as a very generous person, I quite deny.
For evidence, I have only to refer you to the reports
yearly issued by these societies, which usually contain, in a prominent place, a list of benefactors.

Now what does this really mean? What would be thought of a society that professed to exist for the purpose of doing away with drunkenness, but a number of the officers of which were known to be intemperate men, and which was largely supported by saloon-keepers? Would it be credited with much moral earnestness? And, offensive as it may be, I must insist that it is not enough to say of a man that he works hard at his business; it is necessary to ask also whether his business is worth working at, whether it is of any value to society, or whether the activity he displays has for its end, not the adding to the real wealth of the world, but the taking away from other men a portion of what they have created, and putting it into his own coffers.

I asked a fresh-faced young fellow who came to see me some time ago, " What do you do for a living? "

" Oh," said he, " I'm on the stock-exchange."

" Ah," said I, " now will you tell me one or two things about that. Do you think the world is any better off for what you do? "

" I guess not," he replied, " my business is to get all I can from the other fellows."

How widely does that differ from the impostors and tricksters that the Charity Organization Society pursues so indefatigably? No doubt *they* sometimes think they work pretty hard, especially in hot weather, when so many people are out of

town, and so many clergymen in Europe. But
my friend on the stock-exchange would, I am sure,
be accepted as a friendly visitor for the Associated
Charities (he is a church member, and a thoroughly
moral young fellow — when not on the stock-
exchange), and would never hear at the meetings
any remarks about the unrighteousness of stock-
gambling or the immorality of " futures " that
would make him feel uncomfortable.

"But," my friend on the other side remarks,
" do you propose that the Charity Organization
Society should start out on a crusade against all
the doubtful transactions of commercial life ? "

No, I propose nothing of the kind. I only ask
that we should determine, once for all, that we
will be just as outspoken against idleness and dis-
honesty in the mansions and business offices of the
rich, as in the tenement rooms and attics of the
poor. Only let us be under no misapprehension ;
to do that will largely diminish the incomes of
many of the most flourishing charities, and reduce
the salaries of a number of the officers of institutions, and lessen the corps of paid philanthropists
among the poor.

Take another instance. Next to readiness to
work, there is no virtue so universally required of
the poor as fearless and unflinching truthfulness.
This at least we feel justified in demanding of
those on whom we bestow our alms. Few things
bring upon a needy person the verdict " unworthy

and undeserving " so surely and inevitably as false-
hood. No matter how painful it may be to tell a
stranger, the officer of an irresponsible society, the
inner secrets of family life, the things that even
husbands and wives never speak of to each other,
the bitter memories that the heart itself longs to
forget, they must all come out or the risk must
be run of being black-listed in all the cities of
the land. And not *once* only must this be done
but over and over again to a long succession of
" friendly visitors," paid agents, parish workers,
etc.

How would you like it?

This, however, we feel ourselves justified in
demanding under the heaviest penalties for any
indirectness or failure to tell the truth, the whole
truth, and nothing but the truth. Do we consider
that we ourselves can be justly held to any such
transparent frankness? How preposterous! We
don't dream of such a thing.

In our trade, our politics, and a good deal of
our religion, we lie and we know that we lie, and
a good many of us would look with contempt on a
man who should be unpractical enough to suppose
that we can get along without lying. And yet
the very people who are known to be imposing on
their fellow-citizens by their misleading advertisements, their sale of dishonestly watered stock, their
conniving at political knavery, their insincere jour-
nalism, their appeals to men to lay up treasure

in Heaven and get their money's worth at the same time by buying a ticket to a church entertainment, are considered fit persons to hold the poor to the most exact and rigorous truthfulness. To suggest that they are doing under the name of business methods and political expedients and conventional religious trickery something far worse than a poor mother who lies to shield a child from shame, or to prevent her husband from losing his place, would be regarded as very bad taste. Is not the inference plain that the rich are not to be held to the same code of ethics as must be used for the poor?

If still another instance is sought of the fact that even we, who bear the title of philanthropists, assume that the poor are of different stuff from ourselves, let it be found in the way in which we regard their recreations and our own. One of the most damaging statements that can be made against a man whose case is on trial before the committee of a charitable society is that he frequents a saloon. If it can be shown that he sometimes goes home under the influence of liquor he is put in the pillory at once. Possibly some members of the committee think that his wife ought to leave him and put her children in an asylum, and consider her as sharing in his obliquity if she refuses to do so.

Now, without doubt, if we look at the matter from the point of view of our own comfortable surroundings, the frequenting of a saloon is a most reprehensible thing, an exhibition of utterly superfluous wickedness and wanton self-indulgence. That is what it would be for us. Whatever longings we may feel for amusement or for art, for social intercourse or for intellectual entertainment, can all be met in ways that are elevating and ennobling. The impulse that would lead one of us to spend the evening in a saloon could hardly be anything else than a craving for low companionship or for the excitement of drink and play.

But have we any right to assume that because that is true of us it is true of a man to whom all these avenues of enjoyment are closed? Of course the answer made, is that the man we are thinking of has no such faculties of enjoyment as we. And that is just where the limited rationality of our philanthropy shows itself. I do not say that the average unskilled laborer would appreciate a Browning reading or a recital by Paderewski; in all probability he would fall asleep. But this doesn't mean that he has no such faculties as we possess, but that they have not been cultivated and developed. The capacity for the appreciation of Art and Literature and Music are there in that dull mind and that sluggish spirit; and the dim consciousness of powers within him that are not exercised, of a manhood crushed and stifled but living still, is precisely what makes the man crave something beyond the shop where he works and the attic where he sleeps.

Put yourself in his place. Suppose that you

spent ten or twelve hours a day at a perfectly
uninteresting and monotonous trade, in an atmosphere composed largely of carbonic acid gas,
under the eye of a task-master who was paid to
see that every ounce of wealth-producing force
was taken out of you in the course of the day, and
with the knowledge that the least sign of self-
assertion would be visited with prompt dismissal.
Suppose that from the shop you went back, in your
stained and ill-smelling garments, to a room in a
rear tenement where, after a meal eaten at a table
strewed with the dirty plates of various other
persons and lighted with a kerosene lamp, you had
before you the prospect of spending the remainder
of the evening sitting in a room festooned with
somebody else's wash, with no books and no heart
to read them and for your companion a tired wife,
who has nothing but the gossip of the neighbors
to talk about, and is vainly trying to quiet a teeth-
ing baby.

Do you feel sure that such surroundings, week
after week and year after year, would give your
nature all the development it needs? Nothing
of the sort; you are perfectly convinced that
it would be quite impossible for you to do the
work that you feel to be so very important to the
world unless you had an office or studio fitted up
with all the modern improvements, a house in a
pleasant part of the town, books and pictures
and concerts and lectures in the winter and a

trip to the mountains or across the ocean in summer.

Without as much as that you would feel yourself cramped out of all usefulness, you would find no way of realizing yourself. I do not dispute it, but I do maintain that the ignorant toiler has exactly the same impulse to realize himself that you have, and that it is this, — and not mere sottishness, however that may follow in time, — that takes him to the saloon. Once within that enclosure, with a few cents in his pocket, and he suddenly finds that he is something more than a " hand," something more even than an " employé," he is a *man.*

Instead of feeling, as he very likely would at the Free Reading Room ("provided by some kind ladies and gentlemen" who are so intensely interested in the cultivation of literary taste among the poor that they send down their old magazines six months after date of issue and paste up goody-goody pictures out of children's illustrated papers on the wall), that he is a subject of charity and may at any moment find a bevy of his benefactors coming in to show him off to their friends in the interval between a dinner-party and the theatre, he knows that he will be treated with the same deference that his benefactors themselves will receive if they should come in and call for a glass of beer; he knows that he is not on sufferance, that he has his rights and that they will be respected.

There is a good deal of democracy in the saloon even if, in some of our cities, the converse is also true. At the saloon he will find the evening newspaper, he will find men of his own sort ready to talk with him, he will sometimes get a little music, and, if he has a voice, he will be able to take part in a jolly song himself. In other words, the saloon stands to him for what the club, the reception, the Harvard symphony and the Cecilia rehearsal are for us. If we deny it we merely illustrate our need of grasping a deeper sense of human relations. Let no tender conscience think that I have been arguing in favor of the saloon. I know its damning effect, and I have spent some of the best years of my life in urging men to practise the heroism that is involved in staying away; but I see no reason for believing that all the heroism should be found at one end of the social scale and all the easily-gained reputation for virtue at the other.

It seems necessary also to say, that I do not think that the misery wrought by saloons will be removed by the ministers and the philanthropists taking over the business and running it at the old stands, but rather by opening possibilities and pleasures for the poor that will make saloons a superfluity.[1]

[1] " Nothing appears to me at once more ludicrous and more melancholy than the way the people of the present age usually talk about the morals of laborers. You hardly ever address a laboring man upon his prospects in life, without quietly assum-

The many forms of philanthropic industrial education seem beyond reproach ; but here, too, there is a call for a deeper perception of our relation to others in society, and our consequent obligation. For of what value will it be to teach boys and girls any number of trades if we give them no opportunity of exercising them? Of what use is it to have learned to cook, if there is no money to buy

ing that he is to possess, at starting, as a small moral capital to begin with, the virtue of Socrates, the philosophy of Plato, and the heroism of Epaminondas. ' Be assured, my good man,' you say to him, ' that if you work steadily for ten hours a day all your life long, and if you drink nothing but water, or the very mildest beer, and live on very plain food, and never lose your temper, and go to church every Sunday, and always remain content in the position in which Providence has placed you, and never grumble nor swear, and always keep your clothes decent and rise early, and use every opportunity of improving yourself, you will get on very well, and never come to the parish.'

" All this is exceedingly true ; but before giving this advice so confidently, it would be well if we sometimes tried it practically ourselves, and spent a year or so at some hard manual labor, not of an entertaining kind — ploughing or digging, for instance, with a very moderate allowance of beer ; nothing but bread and cheese for dinner ; no papers nor muffins in the morning ; no sofas nor magazines at night ; one small room for parlor and kitchen ; and a large family of children always in the middle of the floor. If we think we could, under these circumstances, enact Socrates or Epaminondas entirely to our own satisfaction, we shall be somewhat justified in requiring the same behavior from our poorer neighbors ; but if not, we should surely consider a little whether among the various forms of oppression of the poor we may not rank as one of the first and likeliest — the oppression of expecting too much from them." — *John Ruskin.*

food or fuel, no land on which to raise wheat, no ground from which to dig coal? Of what use to know how to build bricks into houses, if there are no bricks to be had, and no earth on which to lay the foundations? Can we make good our claim to have exercised a kind beneficence towards these children if we develop faculties in them, and excite hopes, and then refuse to move forward to throw open to them the doors that bar the way to the fruition of those faculties, and the fulfilment of those hopes? And what does that mean but owning that they have as much right to the use of the world as we have ourselves?

I have said nothing of a darker side of organized charity, — of poor men and women hunted down through some stupid blunder, or as the result of some petty malice; questions asked by mysterious persons in heavy veils, questions that stir up a cloud of suspicion round some defenceless girl, who is fighting hard to keep her self-respect and her good name, — this I leave to your imagination. The instances that I know may be rare exceptions. I have a hope that they are, but they are at least not impossible. A stream does not rise higher than its source, and agents are rarely better than the system that creates them. What I deprecate as a menace to philanthropy as a factor in social progress, is an organized charity, — not as it might be, but as in some measure, it has been; not as it is in London, but with us, — an organized charity

that refuses to rise to the higher conception of
men and their relations that the age demands, an
organized charity that remains fixed in narrow
grooves and timid and outworn conventionalities,
an

> "Organized Charity scrimped and iced
> In the name of a cautious, statistical Christ."

As we pass on to College and Social Settlements
we feel that we are breathing a different air. The
spirit that inspires them is not one that is patient
of class distinctions or of effusive expressions of
commiseration for the wretched. There is but
little of the inquisitive temper that led Thomas
Hood to satirize the people, —

> "Who after poking in pots and pans
> And counting garments in want of stitches,
> Have ascertained that the working-man
> Wears a pair and a half of average breeches."

No, College Settlements and Neighborhood Guilds
start out with the conviction that we are all of a
piece, and that shirt-workers, and tobacco-strippers
have natures very much like our own; that what
delights us would, if their powers of enjoyment
could only have a chance to develop a little, delight *them;* that where we go, often with stum-
bling steps, they might, when once they were
accustomed to the way, walk fast and fleet. And
what leads these young men and women to fling
themselves in among the masses of the disinherited

and the despairing, is not that they feel that they owe to them merely pity or prudence, advice or admonition, but that they owe *themselves*, in the bonds of a common kindred and fellowship, in the unity of a common life.

They do not assume to stand upon any higher plane; they come to be taught quite as much as to teach, humbly to ask and receive as well as to offer and bestow. They see that we are never on the terms with a man on which we can do him the highest good until we are as ready to let him do us a favor as to extend one to him. As Mr. Sheldon says, "We cannot help any person unless we can also learn something from him."

And this is not a mere bit of sentiment or pretence; it is the perception of a deep and glorious truth. Some of you I trust have found it out; you have learned that among the poor, among the people who live in narrow courts and crowded tenements, there are riches of reality and simplicity, of unselfishness and love, for which you looked in vain, perhaps, in houses rich with elegance and fair with culture; and in hours of sorrow or disappointment you have been given to feel about you the arms of a warm humanity full of healing and of strength. And yet, those of you who have already engaged in this movement are, I am sure, just the ones to own that you have not reached the goal. Rather, that which stirs you so deeply is the thought of the splendid possibilities that rise before you. Not that there are not times of discouragement; as an old writer says, " He who seeks to serve the poor will have sweet moments and bitter hours "; but that the sense that does come to you, from time to time, of the establishment of such a relation among all men *here*, as many good and holy men have dreamed of as possible only in some future state of existence, recompenses for all your toil. If, then, I seek to point out to you, what may lead us on one step farther, towards that glorious consummation, you will not think that I undervalue what you have already done.

It is yours to recognize in the masses the possibility of pleasure in friendship, of interest in study, of delight in literature, of fascination in science, of enthusiasm in art. You believe that intellectual hunger once roused is more urgent than the hunger of the body; and that men are lifted more surely by exciting that hunger than by simply stuffing their stomachs or training their fingers.

But there is a craving more powerful still; it is the passion for liberty, — not the false liberty of doing one's own will as an individual against the rest of the world but of realizing one's self in closest fellowship with the world. Liberty, true liberty, is not an end in itself but it is a necessary condition of fraternity. We are made for unity, but the unity must be a unity of men, and a man is not fully a man until he is a free man, until the way is open to him for a real self-development, a finding of the law of his being not in things outside of him but in the Divine Reason within him.

So long as I seek liberty for myself alone it will prove a misleading phantom, for my true self is a social self and cannot be achieved in isolation. Unless I am seeking that others may secure freedom I must continue in bondage myself, for others are part of myself. And without freedom even the best gifts, learning, culture, beauty, fail to satisfy. This we all confess, but do we carry it out to its legitimate conclusions? That, and that alone, will establish us in a thoroughly rational philanthropy that will be a factor, will, perhaps, be *the* factor in social progress.

What is necessary to insure freedom for the poor? It is to put them in the position to do for themselves and for others all those things that philanthropy now does for them. Hitherto we have thought of philanthropy as practically the prerogative of a class. Except in those primitive days when classes were unknown, we have taken it for granted that the rich were to be the benefactors, the poor the beneficiaries. But if we are to enter into the new truth that is breaking in upon us (or rather the old truth made young again), that we are all one in Humanity's Head and Lord, that we are members one of another, that we are fellow-heirs of the gifts of God, then we, the educated and refined, cannot any longer wish to monopolize this blessed privilege of ministration and toil and pain for others' good. We shall bid the poor come and work with us for the uplifting of humanity, we may even ask them to come and show us how to work. We shall beg them to consider what we do for them to be only our contribution towards the task in which they, not we, must be the leaders, — the way in which we set them free to do for others what they alone can do.

Is not this the message that Professor Tucker brought to us in such " winged words " in his oration before the Phi Beta Kappa at Cambridge last June ?

" The old idea of working for men is being modified by the larger principle of identification with them. The College Settlement will not supersede the mission, but it will put beside it the broader conception of social unity. . . . It will make service mean, not what we are able to do *for* others, but what we are willing to share *with* others."

Yes, thank God, even the universities, in spite of the academic conceit that so often blinds them, are feeling the impulse of the new life, and are learning to make themselves one with the people. The day of merely helping the poor has for all thinking men long gone by; the day of helping them to help themselves — teaching them in selfish separation to fight, each one for his own hand — is fast waning; the better day of helping them to help others is here.

Does this seem extravagant? Does it seem a kind of indignity to our intellects to suggest that mere artisans and day-laborers may know more about philanthropy than we do, the favored children of this age of culture? And yet the witness of history might well temper our surprise. For, as dear Joseph Mazzini says, " all great national enterprises have ever been originated by men of the people, whose sole strength lay in that power of *faith* and of *will* which neither counts obstacles nor measures time. Men of means and influence follow after; either to support and carry on the movement created by the first, *or, as too often happens, to divert it from its original aim.*"

Books alone will not teach the science of life, and if philanthropy means the simple love for and loyalty to humankind, the poor will still bear off the palm. It is not *they* that build orphan-houses and old people's homes; they open their own doors and bid the outcast to come in. Some little time ago, when I was working among the tenement houses of the East Side of New York, it was not uncommon on entering the conventional three rooms that serve as the domicile of most families, to see the face of a stranger-child among the other children.

" And who is this little girl? " I would say.

" Oh, Father, that's Mrs. Hartman's little girl. Mrs. Hartman had to go to the hospital, and we told Lena to come and stay with us until her

mother gets well. She goes to school with the
other children, and helps wash the dishes."

Or it would be, " Who's that old woman I saw at
your house the other day; is it your grandmother?"

" Oh, no, she's no relation to us ; but she hadn't
any place to stay, and we couldn't bear to turn her
out, and my man said let her stay and do what she
can. She doesn't eat much, and she can mind the
baby while I work on the machine."

Do we think that our asylum-philanthropy will
ever come up to that?[1]

What do you suppose becomes of the poor, the
really penniless and helpless poor, in the intervals
between the visits of the paid agent of the charitable society or the volunteer parish-worker?
Here is a widow, with two or three young children, down sick with pneumonia. The visitor
calls on Monday, and finds the coal and food
almost gone : she sends round a small quantity of
the necessaries of life, enough to last perhaps a

---

[1] If only three families, on the average, in all the congrega-
tions of Christian people in the State of New York would take
in (not as a drudge, but as a member of the household) a single
homeless child, all the orphan asylums in the State, both public
and private, might be closed to-morrow. Could not the State,
if it continues to exempt ecclesiastical property from taxation,
require some such practical fulfilment of the very purpose for
which the Church was founded ? " Whoso shall receive one
such little child in My Name, receiveth Me," is the word of the
Church's Master and Lord. But, alas, it is now as of old, " He
came unto His own [dwellings], and His own [dependents]
received Him not."

day and a half. The "case" slips her mind, or
she goes out of town to see a friend, and it is Saturday before she calls again. Has the poor woman
frozen and starved meanwhile? Oh, no; she finds
her in just about the same condition, but with still
sufficient to live on. Has any other philanthropist
been there? Quite possibly not; only "the woman
up-stairs she came in and brought us some dinner
yesterday, and the baker next door gave my little
girl a stale loaf, and when I was so sick Wednesday night that girl that works in the tailor's shop
across the entry came and sat up with me. Some
of the neighbors do talk about her, but she was
real good, and she says she had a little sister that
looked just like my Minnie, but she died last winter the time work was slack; and the grocer across
the way he said he'd trust me with a hodful of
coals: so we did get along, Ma'am; we poor folks
have to help each other; but if you can do something for us we'd be very grateful."

Wretchedly unorganized, you see; and yet what
a saving of self-respect, and consequently of strength
for future effort, lies in that "we poor folks must
help each other." And may there not be more
real philanthropy in such commonplace, unmeas-
ured, unrecorded acts than in the doles of a bureau
supported by cheques written out in half-con-
temptuous compliance with the wheedling request
of some "society leaders," who have taken to
slumming for a diversion?

The philanthropy of the future, at any rate, will open the way for such deeds on the part of all. It is the way forward to that philanthropy that, in closing this lecture, I ask you to consider. The first step must be to insure to all able-bodied men and women freedom of opportunity to live full and happy lives as the result of their own exertions, and not as the recipients of charity from the members of another class. It will be said, I know, that that freedom of opportunity already exists. I will not weary you with statistics, beyond saying that in 1490 cases of poverty observed by the New York Companies, twenty-nine per cent was owing to an inability to get work; ten per cent to drunkenness.

I only ask if freedom of opportunity to labor exists why is it almost universally considered a favor on the part of a rich man to give a poor man work? The other day a Slav who had been given a job in a Pennsylvania coal mine knelt down and kissed the hand of the boss who set him to work. Neither of them seemed to think the action strange. Perhaps there is nothing for which the poor so often beg as work. I know they do not always want it. There are people that, as wage-workers themselves say, "look. for a job, all the time praying they mayn't find it."

That used to seem to me very reprehensible till one of my boys on the East Side said to me one day, when he had been several weeks looking in vain for something to do, " Father, it frightens

me to be out of work so long. You don't know
how it is with a fellow like us; but if a fellow
that's been working right along loses his place,
the first week he's crazy to get back; he gets up
at four o'clock every morning and looks in the
advertisements, and goes to all the shops where he
thinks they'll take him in, and walks all over town
and up and down both sides of the rivers. And
he does like that the next week and the next, and
he keeps on for one month, or two months, or three
months perhaps; but if he's out of work six months
he never wants to do another stroke of work again,
and that's the way I'm afraid it will be with me if
I don't get a job soon."

However, the fact stands out plain as day that
the poor regard work as a boon; and equally clear
is it that the well-to-do people think they are con-
ferring a favor when they give a man employment.
So habitual is this view of things that we look
upon it as a strange and paradoxical statement
when we are told that the real thanks should be
from the employer to his laborers whom he calls
his "hands." Yet evidently that is the case. For
if the workman did not return to his employer, in
the shape of the product of his toil, more than the
master gives him in wages how could the employer
ever roll up profits, as some employers certainly
do?

Now this fact, that by rich and poor alike, work is
regarded as a gratuity, throws a strong light on the

question whether or not there is freedom of opportunity for all to create for themselves the things they need for life and its delights. Men do not thank their neighbors for allowing them to open their eyes, or fill their lungs, or even cast their votes. There is freedom to do these things. If there really were freedom for men to use their strength to produce what they need, or what they could freely exchange with others with mutual benefit on both sides to procure the things they need, no one would think of thanking his brother for opportunity for working.

But we are far enough from any such state of things as that. Why is it? Well, what do we mean by opportunity to work? Of course we do not mean opportunity for a man to exercise his muscles or to exhaust his physical strength. A man can tire himself out walking along the high-road. But physical labor cannot be long continued without food to supply the waste of tissue, without a shelter in which to sleep, without clothes to protect from cold.

Freedom to work, that is to continue to work, must mean, then, the chance to use one's strength in such wise as to produce food, clothes, the shelter of a house, etc. But it is perfectly clear that all these things, and everything that ministers to man's need, are to be had from the earth and only from the earth. In that sense man is a land animal; he lives on the land and off the

land. Even the other gifts of God are of no use
to him without land. A few miles above the surface of the earth the sun will not warm him, and
the air will not fill his lungs. Out on the ocean
the wind may blow, and the rain may fall, but they
will not ripen any harvests or furnish any fuel
against the cold. Freedom of opportunity means
freedom of access to the land, for land is opportunity. And if the opportunity to work be wanting
it is because access to land is closed.

A single glance into the past will make this clear.
The late Thorold Rogers stands above criticism as
a careful and conscientious historian of the economic
changes of England. He is pre-eminently the statistician, biassed by no prejudice on either side of
the great controversy of the day but simply asking,
" What are the facts of the past?"[1]

In his great work on six centuries of English
labor he declares that in the latter part of the
fourteenth and in the fifteenth centuries poverty such as we are familiar with did not exist.
In that "Golden Age" of labor there was not
one family as poor as seven million people in the
great cities of England to-day. One single con-
trast will suffice. After giving wearisomely minute statistics Professor Rogers sums up by saying that, in the year 1795, the wages of agricultural laborers, judged by the price of food, were

---

[1] This statement is not quite true. Mr. Rogers *began* his
studies strongly opposed to the cause of the wage-workers.

less than one-seventh of what they were in the year 1495. It is wellnigh impossible for us to realize what this means. We only approximate to it, if we imagine what it would be for any one of us to live next year on one-seventh of what he lived on last year.

Now what was the cause of this tremendous change? No sudden and wide-spread exhaustion of the soil is reported; rather, with the introduction of new roots and grasses, the improved system of the rotation of crops, the bringing in of wastes, the development of the quality of live-stock, the land of England had in these three centuries become indefinitely more productive. Not the depreciation of the currency or the statute of laborers; bad as those were they could hardly have produced such extensive misery. Not even the introduction of machinery, as the Socialists would fain have us believe, can be credited with the crime of changing "Merry England" into a land of paupers, in the richest city of which one person in five dies in receipt of public aid. Machinery was still in its rude beginnings and steam-power unknown when the rustic laborers were dying of starvation and the rot.

But one cause remains writ large for those not blinded by the self-interest that vested rights and rent-receiving and landlordism engender. In the two centuries that followed what the peasants still speak of as the "good old times" the land was

stolen from the people, — the opprobrious term is
used deliberately as alone capable of describing the
fact.[1] In the fourteenth century every family had,
or could have, its place upon the soil; there were
commons on which the poorest man could pasture
his goats, his sheep, or his geese, without tax or
toll. But the change of the old military duties
into a money-payment, easily shifted on to the
shoulders of those beneath, had made the ruling
classes of England greedy of land, and little by
little, by stealthy aggressions on the part of individual landlords, or by more open assaults upon
the rights of the people in a parliament controlled
by the landed interest, the common lands have
been inclosed, until now not one person in a thousand in England owns, or can obtain, an acre of
his native soil.

And in the apparently boundless territory of
this American continent the same destructive
forces have been working, only more rapidly, as
would be expected in a new country where the
influence of immemorial precedents and the linger-
ing belief in social duties hardly exist, and where
the sense that natural opportunities are limited in
amount and are being monopolized, makes men
fierce and eager in the struggle. I know very
well there are people who will say that they see
no relation between land-grabbing and poverty;
they don't even see the significance in Ben Tillett's

[1] See " Land and the Community," by the Rev. S. W.
Thackeray, A.M., LL.D., Trin. Coll., Cantab.

epigrammatic utterance: " For every acre of land in England that goes out of tillage one more man knocks on the dock-yard gates for a job." They will say that we cannot all become farmers, and that the poor will not go out of the city even when the chance is given them, and that there are plenty of deserted farms in New Hampshire if anybody wants them, and that if they can do no better they can go West, or that the country is over-populated and that we must limit immigration.

It seems hopeless to try to deal with such arguments as these. It is like attempting to reason with the lady who, in response to your account of the extortionate fines imposed on girls in New York factories, tells you that she is sure things cannot be so bad, because Bridget the cook left her week before last, and she hasn't been able to fill her place yet. But, nevertheless, I will mention two incidents which, if carefully thought out, may show that opening the way to natural opportunities must be the first step in preparing the way for a true philanthropy, if it be not the true philanthropy itself.

Two years ago I was riding down from London to Wiltshire with my friend, William Saunders of the County Council of London. Into the carriage came a nice-looking young farmer, an acquaintance of Mr. Saunders. He farms eleven thousand acres of English soil; of course he does not own it. The conversation turned on a tract of land on

Salisbury Plain. "If I had that piece of land," said the farmer, "I wouldn't take the trouble to till it; labor down there is the most expensive in England" (no wonder, they pay the men nine shillings a week; what work will men do for that?). "If I had that land I'll tell you what I'd do; I'd just put one man on five hundred acres and raise sheep." And that is being done. It is being done in England as it was in Rome two thousand years ago. Consider what it means. Those five hundred acres would support from thirty to forty families of men working for themselves. Our friend proposed substituting one man. What do you suppose will become of the thirty or forty families, that, in the natural course of things, would have found their homes there? They will take the road to London town, to swell the vast hordes that are making the East End the despair of philanthropists and the menace of a nation.

A few months after this I was walking along the road thirty miles west of the city of Philadelphia. I saw in front of me an old man, sixty years of age perhaps; his clothes were old and out of shape, his shoes were dusty and broken; over one shoulder was an old-fashioned carpet-bag and a pair of boots; a heavy overcoat was strapped on his back. As I caught up with him I said, "On the tramp?"

He turned to me with some dignity and said, "No, I'm not a tramp; I'm an old soldier. I fought in 'most all the war, and I never thought I'd be where

I am now. When I left the army I come to Philadelphy and get married. We've alluz had hard luck, and last winter a feller wrote me from Springfield, Missouri, and told me if I liked I could take up one hundred and sixty acres of government land. He said 'twas real nice land, and ef I liked I could take my fam'ly out there in the spring, and by fall I'd have a roof over my head and a place to spend the winter. I reckoned I'd better go out there first and see for myself. So I got enough to take me out there and I went to Missouri. But when I come to locate the tract I see that I'd been took in bad. 'Twas a narrow gulch between two high hills, the sides of 'em was covered with trees and rocks and stones, and 'long the bottom run a stream so scant I had to dam it up to get enough to get a drink. I see right off 'twan't no use to try to make anything out of that, and so I started home; but I hadn't 'nuff to pay my fare. The Mayor of Springfield gave me a ride on a river steamer as far as St. Louis, and then from there I've been walkin' back. It's took me seven weeks; I lived on five cents a day, a half pound of crackers or a stale loaf. Nights I slept out of doors, and if it came on to snow I'd walk on until I got warm again. To-morrow night I'll be home."

Now the point I want you to consider is not whether this story was true or not, though I have partially verified it, but that it might have been true, and that, in that walk of a thousand miles, such a man would pass tens of thousands of acres even in his own State, lying unused under the spring sun, but that he could not have turned a furrow in one of them without being warned off as a trespasser. So back he goes to the city to sink lower and lower in the ranks of the destitute and the poor.

In New York City I know of a number of young men and women among the tenement-house population, who are struggling to get a bit of land and a house for themselves. They join building and loan associations, and with heroic self-denial, set aside from their small earnings one, two, or three dollars every week. One girl said to me, "I'm not going to pay rent to a landlord all my life, if I can help it, and I want to see my father and mother in a house of their own when they get too old to work."

I believe that this determination has been awakened in many of these young people by the fresh air funds which have enabled them as children to go into the country every summer, and so built up in their minds the dream of a fuller, freer life than they can find in a crowded court. I know that when our boys used to come to us at St. Andrew's Cottage, on Long Island, at first we had to beg them to stay. They might have come from the reeking streets of the East Side in sweltering July weather, but even the sea-breezes and open fields had no attraction at first. But when a week was up they would come and ask wistfully, " Mayn't I stay *one* week more? " and, later on, they would want to be there all summer; and, finally, one and another would declare that he meant to earn money and buy a place out in the country, and get his father and mother to move out there altogether.

Alas, very few of them will accomplish it, and every year makes it more difficult. And why? Not because there is not land enough. Within the city limits of New York to-day, there is sufficient space for every family to have its own house. What blocks their way and imprisons them in their caravansaries, is the fact that land near New York is becoming more and more costly every year, is reaching a value that no savings on their part can ever overtake. And yet this increment of value represents no effort on the part of the small number of people who own the land (seven per cent of the whole population), but is the result of the presence in New York of these very toilsmen who, though they have contributed to make the soil of their native city richer than any other part of this country, find that their labor has resulted only in building higher the wall that pens them in.

It is not an answer to say that many of the poor do not care to go out of town, even into the suburbs. I know of many families that have done

so; I know of many more that are trying to do so.
Were the increased values of lands near the city,
which are the direct result of the pressure out-
wards, collected and used for free transportation,
already proved to be a perfectly practical measure,
not only would the holding of land out of use for
speculative purposes be at an end, but the way
would be free for many families anxious to move
away from over-crowded districts to do so at once,
and the stream once started would widen and
grow.   Then the tenement-house wilderness might
once again be glad, and its desert rejoice in open-
ness and air and light.

Our relation with those we meet in our Social
Settlements will not be complete until we can sit
down at their tables as we ask them to sit down at
ours.   But what is felt to be impossible and absurd
in the case of a family living in a tenement, would
be quite possible were the family living in even a
very humble house of its own.

These are only suggestions of the way in which
access to the basis of physical existence, the land,
would insure freedom of opportunity to all.   Into
the deeper economic aspects of the question, there
is no time to enter.   Did space allow, it would not
be difficult to show that the breaking down of the
fundamental monopoly of the sources of production
would provide remunerative labor of one sort or
another to all, and that the standard of wages
would no longer be set by a fierce competition

among the toilers in an unnaturally restricted
area, but by the time and strength it would require
for a man possessed of perfect liberty to produce
and exchange, to support himself on land of ordinary fertility. With freedom of opportunity assured to all, the lazy and shiftless could with
truest kindness be left to the severe but wholesome action of natural laws and to the disciplinary
measure of the State which could then treat pauperism as a crime, and segregate the habitual beggar, for life if it were necessary, as mentally or
morally diseased.

But the breaking down of the monopoly of the
land would have results on others besides the poor.
We are being taught in a great many ways that
society hangs together, and that no one portion of
it can suffer alone. I used to think that the present conditions made the poor wretched and the
rich happy. Less and less does that seem to me
to be true. After spending ten years almost ex-
clusively with the poor, I have of late had some
insight into the lives of the rich, and as I look
beneath the mask of luxury and mirth, I find a
sense of pity and compassion taking the place of
anger and resentment. Edward Carpenter says
that the hovels of East London can only be wiped
out by the destruction of the palaces of the West.
But if "healthy and happy human beings are a
nation's wealth," the call for social reconstruction
is to be heard not alone from Whitechapel, but

from Belgravia; not alone from those who labor, but from those who leech.

It can never be well for any class in the community to be released from the necessity of sharing in the work of the world. Since the abolition of slavery it is land-ownership that creates an idle class. A true philanthropy will care for those who work too little as well as for those who work too much. The philanthropy that will be a factor in social progress will be a philanthropy from which "charity" is eradicated, and which recognizes a universal democracy, not only in politics but in economics, not only at the ballot-box but in the factory and the shop.

V.

PHILANTHROPY AND MORALITY.

By James O. S. Huntington, Order of the Holy Cross,
Westminster, Md.

THERE is a widely diffused notion nowadays
that in our relations with our fellow-men we have
simply to wish them well and to do them good,
and that this is a perfectly simple and easy matter.
The popular demand is for " practical " beneficence
as opposed to a charity based upon " theory." It
is assumed that what sets men at odds is the
fruitless and age-long controversy about " ultimate truths and abstract propositions "; that if
men would only devote themselves to doing good
they would all fall into line, and the sufferings
of the world would be removed. The " service of
humanity " is set forward as a substitute for ad-
herence to creeds and dogmas and formularies of
devotion, or the development of ethical systems.

" Conduct is three-fourths of life," it is said, " and
conduct has to do with people about us. The
outworn theologies of the past have drawn off
the energies of men in vain attempts to know a
God who is by His very nature unknowable, and

fixed the attention of so-called believers on the task of saving their own souls rather than on making this world a little less wretched and needlessly miserable. Why should we any longer hamper ourselves with the uncertainties of religion or the subtleties of a rigorous moral code? Let us go and make the poor comfortable and happy, and leave the affairs of heaven to be attended to when we get there."

Words like these are on the lips of many people in our day and generation. I am sure there is much to justify them. I hope we all sympathize with the spirit that inspires them. I hope we see that it is the spirit of a generous impatience at empty phrases and unreal professions, hollow forms and barren speculations, the spirit of a hearty interest in the welfare of others, and the longing to use one's life in the cause of human improvement. With all this we do well to be in thorough accord. And yet, it is worth while to ask whether there is not an error of thought involved in setting the "practical" against the theoretical, in assuming that men will continue to act unselfishly when the grounds for self-subdual and unselfishness have been forgotten or denied, in believing that a philanthropy that rests on no moral sanction, and is guided by no light but its own, can be a factor in social progress. This is the subject with which we have to deal.

If we press for a definition of the terms " philanthropy " and " morality," we can settle the question in short order. Taking the loose expression "doing good to people" as sufficiently descriptive of philanthropy, it will at once appear that what is meant by the phrase is "doing good to *all* people," not merely benefiting one class at the expense of another; and, of course, the good done must be some permanent and real good, not the gratification of desires for wasteful pleasures or debasing joys.

That is to say, philanthropy, even in its vaguest and most popular meaning, has for its end social progress, the continual development and self-realization of society. But the development of society involves the development of the individuals that make up society, and requires that these individuals should become more clearly conscious of the relations that bind them together, and should voluntarily correspond with those relations. And this correspondence of the individual with the real and necessary relations in which he stands as a member of a universe of self-conscious beings is the very subject-matter of Ethics, or of Moral Science.

Philanthropy requires that men should know themselves as bound together in a unity that imposes mutual services and duties. Morality is the illustration of those duties and the urging them home upon the individual conscience. Philanthropy would not be philanthropy if it did not make for human progress, and the progress of human society is the fulfilment of the moral law.

The individual cannot come to his best save in a society that is moving forward to its true goal, and the advance of society depends upon the development of all the individuals that compose it. Thus a philanthropy that does not contribute to morality is false to its name. We will not linger now to ask more particularly what the conception of morality involves. It will serve a more immediate purpose if we aim to see in some detail how essential it is to bring the efforts of professed philanthropy constantly before the bar of morality, and to show how false is any so-called philanthropy that cannot approve itself there.

One corollary to the position taken can be stated at once. It is this, that *when a fundamental social injustice has come to be recognized and admitted, any efforts towards correcting special evils, that do not contribute to the movement against the underlying wrong, tend to become nugatory and abortive.* If that principle were to be generally accepted, a gauge would be furnished by which we could in some measure test the worth of any philanthropic movement in the direction of social reform and social progress, for all progress is on one side reform, since all progress is a passing out from a lower state of being, that, as the time for the higher state arrives, becomes not merely imperfect, but evil.[1]

[1] Before the Phi Beta Kappa at Harvard last June, Professor Tucker said, "The philanthropy which is content to relieve the

That there is some underlying wrong in our present civilization most of us feel, if we do not openly confess. The growing consciousness of it is the source of a vast deal of the social unrest of the age in which we live. This is as true as that the fact that comparatively few men see where the wrong lies, and who is responsible for it, and therefore how it is to be set right, goes far to explain the confusions and blunders and fruitless struggles in the war between social classes. Still a great deal has been gained in having brought so many of all classes to own that there is a wrong to be righted ; and if, as has just been said, the existence of that wrong is sufficient reason for the failure of the best-laid philanthropic schemes, we who call ourselves philanthropists can with better heart and less desire for concealment bear the exposure of our ill success.

Let us take first, then, the effect of what is to-day recognized as philanthropy upon the recipients of out-door relief. It is one of the axioms of modern charity that the State cannot dispense relief to people in their homes. The ruinous effect of the old English Poor Law, which was in force from 1790 to 1834, has settled that. The fatal effect of State relief in keeping wages below a living point, and in undermining the self-respect and desire for self-maintenance of the working classes,

sufferer from wrong social conditions postpones the philanthropy which is determined at any cost to right those conditions.''

is one of the most familiar themes in the literature of modern sociology. Archbishop Whately says: "Men will do what you pay them to do; if you pay them to work they'll work, if you pay them to beg they'll beg." But even after the mischievous character of State aid had been proved, the notion still held sway that private alms-giving would not pauperize, because, being voluntary, it cannot be counted upon as a certainty or claimed as a right. It was very soon discovered that this hopeful presage had to be modified by adding after " private alms-giving " the clause, "provided that such alms-giving does not overlap, and that investigation of the case is made by the trained officers of the Charity Organization Society."

Yet even with this proviso I believe that the same evils, in somewhat less degree perhaps, will be found to flow from private as from public relief. To those who look at the matter from a distance, the differentiation of private from public charity is easy enough; but to the poor there is probably little sense of distinction between the agent of the city or the county and the paid representative of a large charitable institution, except that one is more distinctly connected with the police in their minds than the other. In applying to both they have to anticipate being asked a great many questions that they don't want to answer and that put a premium on lying,— successfully lying,— and that bar the way to any sense of gratitude. In both cases they imagine that the treasury of the relief agency is practically unlimited, and that if they can only manage to be miserable and poor enough, its mighty forces will be set in motion on their behalf. In both cases the sight of some neighbor-family, apparently as well off as they are, drawing its partial or whole support from public or private alms, excites cupidity while it paralyzes all effort at self-support. And there seems to be hardly any degree of temporary suffering that human nature will not endure with the prospect of getting a living out of somebody else.

In London, we are told, men secure an immunity from work for most of their lives by being periodically run over in the streets by the equipage of some wealthy and soft-hearted person. There are, of course, a great many small societies, of one sort or another, that distribute doles and that are clearly differentiated, even by the poor, from the great relief agencies, either public or voluntary; but these, as developing in the poor the vices of flattery and religious hypocrisy, are not less demoralizing in their effects.

Charity organization has done something to check this particular evil, but there seems little ground to hope that its influence will ever do more than check it slightly here and there. And the mischief spreads far beyond those who succeed in getting helped. The very existence of many of these charitable societies, whether "Associated" or not, is positively baneful and degrading; it keeps before the minds of the poor the dream of a life of dependence on others' bounty; it fosters the preaching of that travesty of the gospel, "alms-giving to the rich, and resignation to the poor"; it invests poverty with a kind of sentimental and sickly romance, and it makes many people, who might otherwise be cheerfully fulfilling the great and sacred law of self-respecting labor, regard their work as a mere misfortune and do their stent with grudging spirit, one eye on their task, the other squinting aside to catch sight of some chance to imitate the higher classes and live on other people. And this very desire is lowering. Mrs. Lowell says, " Human nature is so constituted that no man can receive as a gift what he should earn by his own labor without a moral deterioration, and the presence in the community of certain persons living on public relief has the tendency to tempt others to sink to their degraded level."

" But," it may be objected, " in this sweeping condemnation of philanthropic endeavor to assuage the sufferings of the poor, you must certainly make an exception in favor of the many institutions which, in their various ways, are ministering to those who, as children, or old people, or invalids, cannot possibly take care of themselves." It seems a graceless task to say anything in disparagement

of hospitals and orphan asylums and fresh-air funds
and old people's homes. Few things in this weary
world are as worthy of honor as the tender and loving care of little children, and I hold that there
is hardly any profession or calling so noble as those
of the physician and the trained nurse. Nor do I
suppose that the time will ever come in this earthly
state of things, when certain forms of mental and
moral infirmity, as well as of physical disease, will
not call for segregation in buildings separate from
the homes of the community, and under the skilful
treatment of practitioners specially educated for
the purpose, and furnished with means to do for
their patients what could not be properly done in
their own homes, or in private houses at all.

But I have to deal with the question whether or
not these various institutions, regarded as dispen-
sers of charity, are a blessing or a curse. And, I
ask, is it well that the family, — taking that word
as including near relations, as much as father,
mother, and children, — is it well that the family,
which most of us probably regard as a necessary
factor in social progress, should be relieved of the
support of its dependent members? Is it to the
advancement of morality, — that science and art
of true human relations, — that the poor, the toilers, the ignorant, those who must be taught by life
rather than by books, should be released from the
sense of responsibility for their own children or the
children of their near kindred, of the maintenance

of their own fathers and mothers, or their grand-
parents, of tenderness to the sick and feeble and
imbecile among their kith and kin?   Can we
complacently look forward to a time when only
able-bodied individuals among the working-classes
shall be at large, all the children, sick, and aged
being grouped in institutions called by a kind of
refinement of cruelty and contempt of the divine
appointment of the household, "homes"?

We, in our rank in society, do not consider it
quite the thing to send away from our care and
tenderness those members of our families who
most need that care.   And it is not only for the
sake of those on whom we are so glad to wait.
How much of the sweetness and brightness of our
homes comes from those sick-beds and couches
where lie patient sufferers ready to listen with
loving sympathy to our tales of disappointment
and ill success, bringing to the aid of our ruder
faculties the quickened perceptions of spirits refined by long hours of pain, touching us to nobler
issues, and sending us forth to endure with stouter
hearts, as we carry with us the memory of calm,
pale faces, and the echo of faint but earnest tones.

How many a mother, cut off by ill-health from all
active service, has ruled the hearts of headstrong
boys and wilful girls from her sick-room.   How
many a little child has by its very helplessness
kept soft a father's heart.   Is it well that all this
gracious influence should be taken out of the lives

of the poor? It is of no use to say that the poor
do not appreciate this poetical view of things.
That is not true, to begin with; but if it were, it
would only be an added reason against removing
the very influence by which they may come to
appreciate it.

Or fall back to lower levels and be severely practical. If the desire in our philanthropic endeavor
is to "inculcate habits of providence and self-
dependence," to make the poor diligent in their
work, to give them an interest in the welfare and
advancement of their country, surely it will be
best not to remove from them the very incentives
and motives that in all ages and lands have proved
the most powerful in nerving men to exertion and
effort. The hope in a man's heart of having a
home, whose roof may shelter father and mother
when they are old, and where his children may
grow up shielded from the dangers of the world,
has been a potent factor in the progress of humanity; it has launched ships, and dared tempests,
and felled forests, and conquered fierce and hostile
tribes, and made the American nation.

No philanthropy that weakens this motive, no
philanthropy that does not aim at all costs to preserve and strengthen it, can contribute to social
progress. But what of a philanthropy that erects
Old Men's Homes, and Children's Folds, and Children's Nurseries, and tolerates tenement houses (in
the interest of landlord benefactors), and says

nothing against the robbery from the people of the very earth on which alone their homes can be built? The appeal to men to fight and struggle, and die, if need be, in defence of their hearths, the gray hairs of their sires, and their children's lives, has rarely been made in vain. But what patriotism is to be expected from a man whose wife has died worn out by drudgery in a factory, whose parents are in the almshouse, whose boys and girls are growing up in an institution, and who himself lives from hand to mouth in a room from which he may be evicted in a week if he does not pay his rent? [1]

In the movement of industrial training and Social Settlements there is little danger of pauperization in the ordinary sense of the word, of sapping energy, or of fostering habits of indolence. Yet

---

[1] " It is said that as the first rush was made upon the salient of the Redan, three old soldiers of the 41st Regiment entered with Colonel Windham. The three men were named Hartnady, Kennedy, and Pat Mahony ; the last, a gigantic grenadier, was shot dead as he entered, crying, ' Come on, boys, come on.' There was more in the dying words of the Celtic grenadier than the mere outburst of his heroic heart. The garret-bred ' boys ' would not go on. It is in moments such as this, that the cabin on the hillside, the shieling in the Highland glen, become towers of strength to the nation that possess them. It is in moments such as this, that between the peasant-born soldier and the man who first saw the light in a crowded ' court,' between the cottier and the coster, there comes that gulf which measures the distance between victory and defeat — Alma and Inkermann on one side, the Redan on June 18th and September 8th on the other." — *A Plea for the Peasant.*

one cautionary word may find place. Just so far as, in this sharing with the poor of even the best gifts, we feel that we are doing them a favor, — something that evidences our own magnanimity and for which they are to be correspondingly grateful, — we are allowing the baneful element of " charity " to enter in. We need to remind ourselves from time to time that it would be only a fulfilment of our hopes if a day should come when, as we now establish College Settlements among the poor to teach them music and painting, they will establish Trade Settlements among us, and teach us the altogether noble arts of iron-moulding, weaving, and tailoring. Perhaps by that time there will be some arts they will *not* teach us, because they will have forgotten them as we shall have forgotten our supposed need of them. And in this connection I would remind you of what was said in the preceding paper concerning the Essex Institute in Salem. I have permission to quote the following passage from a very interesting letter sent me by one of the prominent members of the Institute : —

" The Institute has a small fund but its membership contains many wage-earners, carpenters, plumbers, shoemakers, etc., and these members pay their annual assessment just for the purpose of keeping our Institute alive. I do not know as they take· a very active interest in the work at present, although our free lectures during the

winter are attended by people interested in the
subjects regardless of society membership.   The
Institute work is not done, you must know, as a
charity; that is to say, there is no effort made to
lift up what you call the wage-earners, they are
not sought for and brought into the fold to have
historical and scientific information driven into
them, but they come in of their own volition to
help along the good work, and they stand upon exactly the same plane of membership as any one
else.   The gentleman who has now the charge of
the geological department of the Peabody Academy
of Science here was, when he first joined the Institute, interested in botany and was a shoemaker;
he has now given all his time to purely scientific
work.   Another one of our members, who has
become quite a botanist, was engaged in manual
labor, farming, etc.   Another, who is a skilled
microscopist, was a barber.   Of course you understand that they all had the desire which led them
in these directions, and very likely the Institute has
benefited more from them than they from it."

I am sure the workers in the Social Settlements
will feel that they have come very near success
when they can say as much as that.   In the face
of such testimony one feels what a terrible waste
the present condition of things entails upon us in
exhausting, under a ceaseless struggle for mere
existence, men with latent powers, that, if put to
use, might lift the whole world onward.

We take up now the question of the moral
effects of philanthropic institutions upon their
inmates. Of course the most important side of
this question is the moral effect of philanthropic
institutions for children. Childhood is the forma-
tive time; it is then that every touch leaves its
mark. "The child is father of the man," because
the education of the child determines the bent of
the after-life, determines to which of the countless
experiences and impressions that will come to him
he shall give heed, and which he shall ignore
and forget. It is a very common mistake to suppose that only learned people have a philosophy.
If by philosophy we mean a theory of life, some
sort of principle on which facts are arranged, then
there is no one possessed of reason who has not a
philosophy, no matter how unconscious of it he may
be; and it is in childhood that this theory of life is
formed.

It may be thought that the number of children in charitable institutions is too small, and
their influence on society is too weak, to make it
necessary to take them into account in so general
a discussion as this. But social progress must be
judged, not by merely counting heads or considering majorities, but in asking what is the possibility
put before the feeblest and the most obscure to live
a true life and to realize the purpose of existence;
and the number of children under public or private care is not so inconsiderable. In the State of

New York, the number reported last year was twenty-nine thousand. These children will most of them go out into the community and marry; suppose them to have but three children apiece, and you have an aggregate of eighty-seven thousand, who may be expected to show something of the effect of the training that is now being given in the various orphan asylums and protectories of the Empire State. The question is, then, how far does this training make for morality. Of course I do not mean to say that in any case the education is intentionally immoral. I am sure we need not even contemplate such a horrible possibility as that. But that is a long way from saying that the teaching is bringing to these boys and girls all the force of moral example, all the inspiration of moral motive, all the infusion of moral strength, that they need.

The normal environment for the child is the family and the home. It were long to trace the subtle influences that there play in upon a young life, and it is not necessary; we all recognize them as existing : the sense of real and human relations with father and mother, brother and sister, and with a wider circle of those who are akin by blood; the *esprit de corps* of the household to which the child feels that he belongs and in which he soon begins to form an appreciable factor; the finding a basis for authority in one who is the author of his life; the chivalry called forth in the protection

— even only the fancied protection — of mother and sister ; the care and teaching of younger children ; all these are as natural as air in the true family, but there is only the faintest shadow of them in the institution.[1] Of course there is a great difference between one and another form of asylum.

Where nine hundred boys, no girls, all of about the same age, or, if of different ages, divided up and kept apart, the older from the younger (a measure that is often, no doubt, necessary, though the very necessity only serves to show the unnatural effect of institution life), are brought together in one enclosure, taught and worked in gangs, turned out to play by scores or hundreds, put to sleep in dormitories where the long lines of beds stretch like lines of graves on either hand, — where the very names of the boys are laid aside and they are known only by numbers, where they are dressed alike, taught alike, fed alike, and when they appear in public form but units in a procession that excites the curiosity or the contempt or

---

[1] It is strange that even those who own allegiance to One Who has reconsecrated and re-established all the faculties of human nature, and all the ties that bind society together, should, under the warping influence of a spiritual domination, attempt to stifle some constituent of the common humanity. A while ago a father went to take his little girl from the protectory where she had been for some months. On their way home the child hung behind her father and would not look up at him. He finally elicited the explanation, — "The Sisters say it's wicked to look at a man."

the pity of the passers-by, — there the very principles of the family and the home seem to be not
only forgotten, but reversed.

This trying to bring up children by machinery, indeed, is slowly disappearing, and a more
rational method is taking its place. Here the children are broken up into groups in which those of
different ages live together in a house with an
older person as its head, and the older ones have
even rooms of their own and some sense of individual personal possession ; here there is at least
the simulation of family relations and a possibility
of the growth of mutual loyalty among the members of the little group, and so of gentle affections
being developed.

But still, at the best, it is almost out of the question to attempt to give these children anything of
that feeling of responsibility for the maintenance
and welfare of the asylum that nearly every child
has for the support of the home, and that does so
much to draw forth the energy of the growing boy
or girl and make life and its interests, the household and its needs, the family and its relations,
keen and vital and vivid in a child's mind.   The
" charity-child " (what a mockery the name is !)
accepts his support as just as much a certainty as
the course of nature ; he expects his food and
clothing as he expects day to follow night; he
knows that he does nothing, can do nothing, need
do nothing, to provide for his physical wants, and

grows up to look upon his tasks as a more or less disagreeable necessity, for which he sees no particular reason in the nature of the world about him.

Quite possibly he does not handle money at all; certainly he has very little opportunity to know the worth of commodities, to understand that labor gives things value, and that price is in some degree the measure of work. Thus he knows nothing by practical experience of the processes of production or distribution, and grows up in a world as little like the one into which he will have to go out as Mr. Bellamy's fabled Utopia is unlike the world of to-day. Yet even that comparison is unfair, because Mr. Bellamy assumes that his socialistic state will be the creation of its members, that *all* the children will grow up under its paternal care, that therefore none will feel that they are cared for by the State as an act of grudging beneficence to the young of a dishonored and disinherited class. Under such conditions private charitable institutions for children would be unknown, and the debasing sense of entering upon life as a pauper would be rendered impossible.

Opposed as I am to that system which is known among us as Socialism, superficial as I believe its remedies to be, and impossible as I conceive it would prove to carry them out, without involving us in conditions yet more intolerable, yet I do not consider it in any way a part of my function in the world to apologize for the existing disorder and wrong. And while I acknowledge that voluntary philanthropic institutions for children often have many advantages over public institutions for the same purpose, it seems to me that they labor under one almost fatal difficulty: they are supported entirely by those whose interest it is that the existing social and industrial maladjustment should continue; they are, therefore, on the side of the very system that makes orphan asylums necessary.

The trustees and patrons and patronesses of the Home appear to the child as a kind of earthly providence, as beings from another world, who shower their gifts upon their suppliants beneath, and occasionally descend in their chariots with wonderful attendant angels in livery, to receive the admiring glances and grateful smiles of their clients, perchance to confer upon some particularly attractive child a kind of patent of nobility by some special notice and condescension. If anything were needed to enhance the child's reverence for these heavenly visitants, it would be found in the deep reverence and obsequious servility with which their advent is anticipated and their favor sought by the authorities of the asylum, who at other times seem to the childish mind to be possessed of wellnigh unlimited power.

What is the effect of this sort of bringing up? In the minds of the many, to generate a feeling of dependence and unreasoning submissive-

ness to anybody who wears good clothes and
rides in a carriage, — a dispirited acquiescence
in life-long inferiority to the rich, — this in the
minds of the many; in a few of the keener and
more intelligent, whose elasticity of mind prevents them from being reduced to a dull conform-
ity of opinion, the result is an attitude of silent
but bitter antagonism, — a warped and distorted
view of society, under the influence of which they
will look upon the rich as their natural enemies
and oppressors. These two classes can be found
in almost every large orphanage. While they remain there the characteristics do not show themselves, save in exceptional cases; there is an institutional morality, just as there is an institutional
health, the children seem to be obedient and well.

But there is no foundation of moral or of physical strength; they have grown up like plants under cover; once out in the open where the sun
shines hot and the wind blows free, and they wither
or bend. The members of the first class become the
helpless victims of circumstances; they drudge
through their work in a dreamy and exasperatingly
complacent fashion, equally unresisting and uninteresting; the nerve, the snap, the spring, seem to
be gone; they feel a constant and depressing sense
of inability to cope with a world so different from
any they have ever known; its rough, irregular
ways, its freedom and spontaneity, perplex them;
they yield to cruelty or oppression without dream-

ing of opposing it; they resort to the weapons of
the weak, — deception, secrecy, and reserve; if
they are girls they are easily led astray, not
always, by any means, through inherited taint or
native badness, but from a long habit of unthinking
surrender to any one who seems to be above them.

If father or mother be living, that strange mysterious bond between parent and child may assert
itself, and once more unite them to the world; but
if there be no close relatives, the years in the
ayslum have probably made too deep a breach
between them and more distant kindred for the
tie to mean anything in particular. Thus they
are really adrift in the world, and they naturally
become the dupes and victims of the aggressive
and determined among either the rich or the poor.
After a few years they find their way back to institution life again, — only this time it is the peni-
tentiary, the reformatory, or the workhouse, instead
of the orphan asylum. Poor, helpless sheep, fleeced
and shivering, it is like getting into the fold again.
If the fare is coarser and the regimen stricter, they
themselves are coarser and harder to stand it.
Once more they can throw off responsibility for
food, or lodging, or raiment; once more the regular hours break up the day, and bolts and bars,
though they limit locomotion, assure them of the
uselessness of being anything but machines.

The race run by those of the second class, — the
bolder spirits, — is usually shorter still. Society

has, as they think, thrown down the gage to them, and they take it up. Life is for them a desperate struggle for reprisals from the community which has robbed their childhood of a home. In the orphanage they were the leaders in any scheme of mischief that was from time to time attempted; in the world they find a larger field for their ingenuity and daring. They become, if men, the dangerous criminals, the marauders and cut-throats, the sturdy beggars and more reckless tramps; if women, the adventuresses and betrayers of other women. But society usually proves too much for them, and has them under lock and key before long, giving them a chance to recover from dissipation, and devise new schemes of deviltry when their term in prison is over. In one respect, both classes are alike; the sense of corporate life, of oneness with humanity, of fellowship is wanting; and so the very foundation and groundwork of morality has not been laid.

I am perfectly aware that facts will be adduced to show that I am unjust in this description; I should be unjust if I meant to assert that all " charity children " go to the bad, or that there are not in almost every institution counterbalancing influences that often materially modify the tendency of the system to drag down the inmates, and so largely neutralize the evil. As there are in almost every religion men better than their creed, so there are in every form of philanthropy men and

women better than the system they represent and
administer.   There are in children's homes teachers
and keepers who pour out a wealth of love upon
their charge, and win them to goodness by the
beauty of it in their own words and deeds, — who
build up even in these tardily responsive natures
the sense of a wide and all-embracing love, — a
love that encircles and unites humanity, because
it is the presence in humanity of God, the Infinite
Love.   There are ties of affection that prove as
firm and lasting as ties of blood.   All this is true;
I rejoice that it is; but we cannot judge of the
effect of an institution by that which is accidental
to it.   That was the sort of reasoning that forty
years ago justified chattel slavery, owing to exceptional instances of benevolent masters who
made their slaves happy and tried to make them
good.

In my description I have aimed to bring before you, what is the legitimate outcome of the
system where other elements do not come in to
interfere.   Those of you who are familiar with the
history of English orphanages will know that the
picture is not a fancy sketch.   Most of us have
not quite forgotten our "Oliver Twist."   And it is
the calm conclusion of many modern philanthropists that any home, however poor, even if it is
not entirely clean, — any home, so long as it is not
actually vicious, — is a better place for a child to
grow up than the most perfectly appointed and

well-regulated orphan asylum, furnished with all
the modern improvements.[1]

[1] After the above passage was written my father (Bp. Huntington) called my attention to the following colloquy in "Beggars All," by L. Dougall (Longmans, Green and Co.), a book
marked by a delightfully clear style, an undaunted faith in
God, a lively play of wit and many penetrating observations
upon character.

"'A child left destitute upon the world is a wailing conun-
drum. Some people would answer by killing it, and some by
putting it in a charitable institution. I don't know which is
best. I was such a child myself.' . . . He spoke out of a deep
lifelong indignation, not temperately or wisely, yet as he spoke,
Star could not help feeling sympathy with him. . . . 'Whenever children are brought up on public money,' said Hubert,
'there is, as far as I know, a matron, and a committee to see
that she does her duty, or what is equivalent to that. Who is
the matron? Take the best mother that ever lived, and set
her to bring up her family in obedience to the dictates of a
dozen self-important aunts and uncles, who visit frequently and
are free to criticise and alter whatever they please, and tell her
to keep her house open for an hour or two every week that the
public may go through and write letters to the newspapers —
how do you think it would work?' He paused a moment, let-
ting his question sink into her mind. 'Would that be a position that any true mother on this earth would choose?'

"'No,' said Marian wonderingly, 'I think not.'

"'No; and the women who hold that position toward other
people's children are shallow, or callous, or base, or a mixture
of all three. But, whatever their character may be, they and
the children must live a life in which the look of things is everything, for it is by the look of things they are judged, and all that
is mean in human nature is developed by it. You can't mend
the matter. Give the matron more power, and ten to one she
abuses it. All I say is this — take the most motherly woman
in the world, she can't fill the position as it is; alter the posi-

The course of our considerations has just led
us to refer to reformatory institutions for adults.
Most of these lie beyond the limits of voluntary
philanthropy; there are no private institutions
that receive men for purposes of reformation except a few inebriates' homes. But there are a
good many penitentiaries, Houses of Mercy, Shelters, and other places of safe-keeping for women.
Of the need of these reformatories there can be no
doubt. And they form an entirely proper field for
private charity.

As we have noted, private beneficence can make

tion, and you run the risk of getting the worst women in the
world into it. The system is bad.'

" ' But you, Mr. Kent, you have come out of the ordeal
unscathed.' Marian smiled. Her tone suggested that he
must exaggerate the evil. ' You are a contradiction to your
words.'

" Hubert laughed and, on the whole, his laugh was self-
satisfied.

" ' They did n't take me off the streets till I was six, and the
Jesuits say that the first six years are final, so my sins and
virtues need not be set down to charity. But I tell you, Miss
Gower, one thing that saved me from being a knave was the
honest indignation that was roused in me every day at the
orphanage. The rich folks had given their money to buy
the satisfaction of feeling charitable. How they enjoyed their
purchase! And the machine they were so busy oiling and
polishing was grinding out dullards and sneaks. I fought
for the dullards, and worked off my badness that way, and
I resolved that I would fight against the class that patronized
us ; and I'll do it as long as I live. I'd rather stand to-day
before the world with Montagu, the lamp-lighter, as my friend
than go dining with any of the managers of that orphanage.' "

ventures and institute experiments that the constituted authorities in a democratic state are not
free to undertake. What is aimed at by charity
of this sort is reformation of character. I am
sure that in many instances great improvements
result. Two remarks seem called for by the
facts as they are known to me. The first is that
a true philanthropy must recognize that punishment is a factor in the establishment among men
of a robust and rational morality. There is a good
deal of danger at present from the existence of
a weak and sentimental pseudo-philanthropy, that
looks upon criminals as heroes, and grades its
admiration by the heinousness of their crimes.

The statement is openly made that the State
has no right to punish offenders, and that all restric-
tive laws are an encroachment upon human liberty.
" Sin," " crime," " vice," these are regarded as outworn and meaningless terms; those who do wrong
are viewed as the victims of an unfortunate and
an unpropitious environment; restraint, it is said,
is what incites to actions that make the world
unhappy; remove all barriers, abolish all discipline, and everybody will be good. This anarchis-
tic hypothesis may not be distinctly formulated
by persons who condemn punishment and send
bouquets to murderers, but the mistake that is
present to their minds is that which underlies
anarchism, that society as organized in the State
is the subversion of liberty and the antithesis of
rights.

On the contrary, freedom, human freedom, is possible only in society, and the State is the realization of rights. We see this if we remember that freedom is only to be predicated of persons, and that personality implies and necessitates relations, and relations with men can only be had in society. The State is the ordering of those relations as against the disturbing and divisive forces of brutish selfishness and irrational self-will. Sin (of which crime or an infringement of the laws of society is a manifestation) is selfishness, the making self the centre and self-will the rule of the universe. In order to the preservation of liberty the State must have the power of educating its citizens out of the fatal error that is involved in thus traversing the law of the *cosmos*, and the power of unveiling the true nature of crime by imposing its consequences upon those who yield to it.

Thus arises the right to threaten and to inflict punishment. The State must teach its citizens that penalties are attached to the infraction of the laws that declare the obligations of men to each other, and must impose the penalties in case the laws are broken. The most fitting penalties are those which consist in segregating criminals from the company of their fellow-men. This act is an emphatic declaration that the prisoner has already severed himself from the common life by yielding to the impulse to disregard and

despise the relation that bound him to his fellows.
If rightly inflicted, with no partiality shown to
wealth and no advantage taken of weakness, such
punishment might awaken in the wrong-doer the
sorrow for his misdeed, and the longing for resto-
ration to right and true relations again. If the
human relation has been wilfully and wantonly over-
thrown by taking the life of another human being,
the fit consequence is permanent separation from
society by life-long imprisonment if not by death.

Punishment, then, not only is an effort on the
part of society to protect itself, nor only for the
reformation of the offender; it must aim at both
these results. "Society never has claimed, and
does not now claim, the right to punish for an
infraction of the moral law. . . . The fundamental principle upon which man assumes the
right to punish his fellow-man is that society, as a
whole, may be protected. It is, therefore, clear that
any act done that is not necessary for the protection of society, and which does not tend to protect
society, is unwarranted and wrong." [1] And unless
punishment seeks the deliverance of the culprit
from the tyranny of the vicious impulses or habits
that led him to commit the crime, society becomes
guilty of producing or continuing the source of the
very offence it chastises.

None of us, I suppose, are doubtful that our

[1] "Our Penal Machinery and its Victims," John P. Altgeld,
Governor of Illinois.

prison-system, our whole penal machinery, fails
wretchedly of repressing crime or reforming character. As Mr. Altgeld says, "it seems, first, to
make criminals out of many who are not naturally so; and, second, to render it difficult for
those once convicted ever to be anything else
than criminals; and, third, to fail to repress those
who do not want to be anything but criminals." So long as this is the case there will be
a fruitful source of the present weak and mischievous compassion for thieves and ruffians. Notwithstanding this, we must not allow an ignorant
and emotional philanthropy to impede and render
nugatory what little really educative and corrective punishment we have. There are soft-hearted
persons who would cry out in the name of philanthropy against indeterminate and cumulative sen-
tences, and still more against the incarceration for
life of vagabonds who have never done anything
worse than go on in beggary, dirt, and drunkenness, and beget children doomed by their birth to
idiotcy, profligacy, or crime. Yet the sterilization
of the unfit by life-long segregation is demanded
in the interests of every hope of social morality,
and it is a blot upon our civilization that men and
women should be sent to the Island or the Bride-
well, a dozen times a year for ten days or two
weeks at a time, year in, year out, from their
first commitment for drunkenness at eighteen or
nineteen years of age, till they stumble at last into

a pauper's grave. What a senseless mockery of corrective discipline to suppose that a drunkard of forty years' standing is going to be reformed by giving him ten days at the Island for the hundredth time!

The second suggestion I desire to make is, that the philanthropy which attempts to uplift these victims of self-indulgence and self-will must depend very largely upon awakening and stimulating the social instinct, upon exciting the impulse to do something for others. Mental and moral aberration are nearly allied: in one the mind, in the other the will, is centred upon self; but the line between them often eludes the most discerning scrutiny.

Our modern method of treating insanity is to seek to draw the patient out of his isolation, to bring him into natural and healthful relations with others. In our dealing with moral disease this has not been used as much as it will be by and by. Where it has been tried the results have often been beyond expectation. Why should they not? Is not man raised rather by the power of self-sacrifice that links him with God than by self-interest that likens him to the brute? Is it not due to its appeal to this desire to help others that the Salvation Army, crude and vulgar as it is, and wretchedly individualistic as is its theology, has won its real and substantial victories among the dissolute and depraved? No sooner was the attention of some poor wretch caught by the beating drums and singing lassies, and some secret spring in his heart touched by a plaintive voice and the pressure of a kind hand, than he was set to work to do what he could for one of his companions in misery.

In the summer of 1890 I was in London, and went with Commissioner Smith, then at the head of the Social Wing of the Army, to a work-yard in Whitechapel. We reached the yard — a small open space in the midst of a number of rough buildings — a little after noon. A boy in the red shirt of the Army opened the wooden gate, and we passed in under a covered archway. The first thing I saw was a group of fifty or sixty men gathered under the open sky in the middle of the yard, kneeling each on one knee, while one of the officers led the noon prayer-meeting held in all Salvation Army barracks and work-yards. As the crowd rose at a sign from the leader, I looked into their faces. Then I realized the desperate character of the work attempted: misshaped figures, pallid cheeks, lack-lustre eyes, gaping mouths, the scars of want and sin. Could anything be done for such as these?

Among them one man was pointed out to me, a jail-bird, who had spent under lock and key forty years out of his sixty-odd. The keeper of the yard — a quiet, unassuming man — told me that this old fellow had come in the week before with another man. His companion, after a day or two, got out of temper with one of the officers, and was discharged. When the old convict heard that he was gone, he went away and put his arm up against the wall and hid his face in it and cried like a child. After a time he came back to the keeper and asked permission to go out and try and find the wanderer and give him another chance. The next Saturday night the permission was granted, and about ten o'clock he came back, bringing the other man with him, his poor, bad old face all aglow with a new-found enthusiasm, — the enthusiasm of humanity.

Suppose, for a moment, that that could be carried out on a grand scale; imagine some mighty movement that would lay hold upon the weakest and the worst and gather them up and send them forth to save their fellows, might there not be found a moral motive power that would be strong enough to lift men above themselves, above the cravings of their appetites, above their selfishness and their sin? And that is what must be sought by the new philanthropy.

We used to stop with the negative half of the apostolic counsel, and say merely, "Let him that stole steal no more" (applying that, too, to small thieves, not to great ones; to men who stole bits of railroad iron, not to men who stole railroads; to those who stole the goose from the common, not who stole the common from the

goose); we did a little better when we went on to
say, "but rather let him labor" (though we were
not wisely careful to see that opportunity to labor
was set free); we did better still when we learned
to add, "working with his hands the thing that is
good," and taught the manual arts; but now the
spirit of the coming age is calling us to go forth
even to the cadger and the crook, — for they, too,
are men, — and bring to them the nobler summons
of the full message, "Let him that stole steal no
more, but rather let him labor, working with his
hands the thing that is good, that he may have to
give to him that needeth."

That has, indeed, a ring about it that may well
stir the dullest soul, for it makes the hard struggle
against low desires something more than an exchange of one form of selfishness for another. But
the call must come, not from the lips of two or
three alone, but with the thunder of a great
multitude, strong with the hope of a new and
better world.

Leaving what has been said as merely illustra-
tive, in a few instances, of how modern philanthropy fails to minister to the moral life of its
beneficiaries, we must turn, if only for a moment,
from considering the effects of alms-giving on the
recipients to contemplate its results on its dis-
pensers. One of the most patent facts about this
side of the matter is, that the charities of the rich
are an insurance which they pay for the security

of their possessions and the continuance of their gains. Of late years the premium has risen somewhat, but the policy is still good. I do not mean to say that many people actually sit down to figure the thing out; but there is a sense of added security for wealthy people, " a soothing of their conscience and a calming of their fears," in knowing, or having reason to believe, that the poor are not quite starving.

In the Middle Age, red-handed barons gave away large moneys to the poor out of their ill-gotten stores, in order to relieve their anticipations of reprisals made upon them in the *next* world; to-day, men do very much the same thing in view of possible reprisals in *this*. That is not in accordance with a very high morality; it is a contemptible combination of cowardice and greed. But worse still is the assistance to wilful ignorance and self-deception that alms-giving furnishes to the donors. The temptation to juggle with one's conscience is not, of course, confined to the rich; but it attacks them in particularly subtle and alluring forms. There is so much at stake in the case of one possessed of a great deal of money, and the position in the world that that assures; to be brought to acknowledge that one's wealth is the result of injustice, even if were not one's own, would lead to such frightful consequences; to confess that one is living on goods stolen from the very poor that it is so pleasant to

patronize would be so horribly humiliating; and
to think of surrendering one's property would
entail such social obloquy and involve the loss of
so much social esteem, — that we cannot be surprised that people of this class instinctively close
their minds to any argument that might lead to
such painful conclusions.

This is a sufficient explanation of the way in
which men and women in the higher classes
cling to some exploded theory like that of Mal-
thus, and repeat some mere sophism that an un-
biassed mind would dismiss at first sight. Hardly
a week passes that we do not hear some feebly-
stirring conscience, vaguely uncomfortable at foolish and wasteful luxury, lull itself to sleep again
by repeating the well-worn formula, "Oh, well, it
gives the poor work and keeps them from starving." If sarcasm is ever allowable, it certainly is
in meeting such mere salvings of conscience as
this. It would seem to be one of the occasions
to which the Scripture refers when it says, "Answer a fool according to his folly." The following
lines may not be familiar, they seem apposite:

"Now, Dives daily feasted and was gorgeously arrayed, —
  Not at all because he liked it, but because 't was good for
    trade;
  That the people might have calico he clothed himself in
    silk,
  And surfeited himself on cream that they might have more
    milk.

He fed five hundred servants that the poor might not lack
bread,
And had his vessels made of gold that they might have
more lead;
And e'en to show his sympathy with the *deserving* poor,
He did no useful work himself, that they might do the
more."

Now if this temptation to lend one's self to a
pleasant delusion exists in some special degree
among the rich, it would seem a duty to avoid
anything that might add strength to the temptation. But this is just what the philanthropy of
our present state of things does. It enables
wealthy men or women, without stinting themselves of a single thing that ministers to their
comfort or enjoyment, to smother, under a host of
benefactions and charities, the voice of conscience
calling them to accept some unwelcome truth.
Worse than this, these very charities draw forth
a chorus of flattery and adulation, until the person
is fairly bespattered with praise. The owner of fifty
million dollars, whose imagination has been impoverished by the very vastness of his possessions, —
though in reality he does not possess them and
never can, — and who cannot find a way of spending, on his own gratification, a tenth of his income,
gives fifty thousand dollars to a philanthropic object. Such a donation makes no appreciable difference in his comforts or even his luxuries. It is
no more to him than fifty cents would be to some of

us; but the man is lauded to the skies for his "deed of noble self-denial," and accorded the freedom of the city. It is very hard not to believe that what everybody says about you is true, especially when it is something that eases your conscience, and makes you think yourself a remarkably fine person. This we reckon as another way in which modern philanthropy does not contribute to morality.

It were too long a task to enter into all the ways in which a philanthropy that will not acknowledge the fundamental iniquity of present conditions leads to other immoralities as well, but here is one other. While freely it is owned that many strikes are unjustifiable and wicked, it is not often confessed that there is about almost every strike a great deal that is heroic, unselfish, and, therefore, highly moral. Think of it. Here is a set of men receiving the highest wages in their trade, who for the sake and at the call of men they have never seen — men who have never done anything for them, and who they have reason to think would do nothing for them in like circumstances — are ready at a moment's notice to quit their work, their only means of subsistence, and face poverty and hunger, some of them, perhaps, imprisonment and death. How many rich men would do as much for their dearest friends? But philanthropy, the philanthropy of the present, has no sympathy for such morality as this. It never stops to ask whether the strike is not for a righteous cause, — whether it may not have arisen, as I have known to be the case, from a demand for the discharge of a foreman who had seduced one of the factory-girls, and was trying to seduce another, — but condemns all strikes indiscriminately, and refuses aid even to the women and children who have had no part in the matter. I said that all philanthropy did this ; I am glad to say *that* is not true. During the great dock-strike in London in 1889, the Oxford University Mission in the East of London did a large relief-work among the strikers, and thereby lost a number of rich friends and gained a great many poor ones. (I would remind those who do not agree with this part of my paper that the Church has not often of late erred in this direction.)

Nor is this all. Much modern philanthropy not only fails to recognize the morality involved in men standing by each other in resistance to what they believe to be unjust on the part of the corporations that exploit them, but deliberately declares that to qualify himself for the receipt of charity a man must throw overboard any regard for the industrial welfare of his fellows, and be willing to work for the benevolent society or philanthropic individual for less than other men in the same trade are working, for less than would afford a self-respecting man a livelihood. And, not satisfied with this, many philanthropic institutions,

especially those which profess to be of a religious .
character, pay their servants and employés less
than the majority of laborers receive for like service, have their buildings erected by "scab" brick-
layers, and their printing done by "bum" printers.

There are many shams in our modern religion-
ism. I know of few more loathsome than the hypocrisy of the lady-managers (what a singularly
suggestive title!) of an orphan asylum worth a
half a million of dollars, who expect a hired nurse-
girl to be content with less than a private family
would pay, because she is working, as they say,
"for the Lord,"—so afraid that she will not lay
up sufficient treasure in heaven that they rob her
of half her wages on earth, and, while they tell her
in unctuous phrases that "it's all for the good of
the dear little children," neglect to print her name
among the benefactors of the "institootion,"
though the proportion to her income of what she
perforce contributes entitles her to head the list.

Many of the trustees of such "Homes" profess
an unbounded faith in the Bible. It would be well
for them to show by their works that they believe
that "God loveth a *cheerful* giver," and that the
denunciation upon "those who build their houses
by robbery and their chambers by wrong," in the
under-payment of carpenters and masons, was not
written only for Jews of three thousand years
ago.

But it is time that we stopped and asked, "What

if all this is true? What cure do you propose? Or do you want to abandon all charitable efforts and let things take their course, and natural laws work themselves out in their own relentless way?" I believe that morality must precede philanthropy. Before we can do good we must do right. We must hunger and thirst after justice before we can be merciful. It is not that, as the old lumbering, Calvinistic theology taught, Justice is opposed to Mercy, but that Mercy without Justice will not be Mercy, even as we cannot really do good unless we are striving to do right. " The tender mercies of the wicked are cruel," says the Bible, and it has been proved true over and over again. If we ignore the right and start out merely to do good to people, we shall before long make ourselves the judges of the good; we shall be saying (how many a philanthropist has come at last to say it!), " These people do not know what is really good for them, but I do; and if they will not voluntarily take what will do them good, and is meant to make them happy, I will see that they do so under com-. pulsion." And when that has once been said there is no atrocity that may not find shelter under so specious a pretext. And from those who go forth to their fellows with the intent of forcing upon them the selfish conceits of their own minds, may a God of justice deliver His bleeding and defence-less children!

The first thing to settle clearly, then, is that

we must first of all be right ourselves, and then do the right regardless of consequences. This is, and has been, and forever and ever will be, the best thing for rich or poor, for high and low. It may be that the doing of the right will bring sorrow and pain upon us and upon others; but the mere escaping from present misery, or the saving others from it, is not the best thing for them or for us.

The author of that most painstaking book, " Life and Labor of the People in East London," has one sentence so sad and yet so unflinchingly true that it will serve to illustrate what I mean better, perhaps, than anything else at hand. The paragraph is headed " Dr. Barnardo's Homes." It reads as follows : " The work of Dr. Barnardo is most remarkable. There is, I believe, nothing in the world like it. I need not describe either his methods or their results. They are well known. With its motto, 'Save the Boy,' a large and symmetrical structure has been built up, stone by stone, each stone an individual case of child-destitution. The only remark I would offer is that, with such dimensions as Dr. Barnardo's work has assumed, special dangers show themselves. His intervention may begin to be counted on, and, if so, it will finally stand convicted as the cause of misery."

To say that we must put morality before philanthropy is, after all, to repeat in other words

what has been said in the preceding paper, that
we must infuse into our emotional philanthropy
the element of a true rationality. When we have
come to recognize that there is a Divine Purpose
in the world, that a great plan is working itself
out, then we shall be more anxious to have our
whole lives, our thoughts as well as our deeds,
brought into harmony with it, than to engage in
well-meaning efforts that may turn out to be rather
a hinderance to the true order than a help. We
must not try to cure symptoms, but attack the
seat of the disease, even if we find it in our own
hearts. This is what Henry Thoreau taught us
thirty years ago. "He felt," says his latest biog-
rapher, Mr. Salt, "that philanthropy is not love
for one's fellow-man in the broadest sense ; not the
flower and fruit of a man's character, but only the
stem and the leaves; not the constant superfluity
of his benevolence, but a partial and transitory act
in which there is frequently too large an admixture of self-consciousness." Then, quoting from
Thoreau, "there are a thousand hacking at the
branches of evil to one who is striking at the root,
and it may be that he who bestows the largest
amount of time and money on the needy is doing
the most, by his mode of life, to produce the
misery which he strives in vain to relieve. Some
show their kindness to the poor by employing
them in their kitchens. Would they not be kinder
to employ themselves there?"

Agreement is assumed, then, in the proposition that we must *be* right and *do* right in order to *do* good; that if "Conduct is three-fourths of life," Character is the whole of it.

But Right is founded upon Truth; it is the Truth gone into operation. Now the Truth that underlies our actions towards others is the relations we hold with others. What we can all do at once is to awake to a consciousness of these relations and begin to correspond to them in our dealings with the cook and the waiting-maid, the clerk and the cash-girl, the railway conductor and the telegraph-boy, the factory-operative, the dressmaker, the newspaper reporter, as well as the beggar and the charity "case."

When a distinguished visitor told an amusing story at Charles Kingsley's dinner-table, after laughing heartily at it Kingsley turned abruptly to his wife as though a sudden thought had occurred to him, and said, "My dear, I'm sure that Mary would enjoy that story very much; will you ring for her to come up? I know that Mr. So-and-so won't mind telling it again." Not only the obligation, but the joy, of thus entering into natural and real relations with others, rather than trying to create artificial and strained relations as dole-dispensers and friendly visitors, is being brought home in many ways to many hearts. When we have learned to value the friendship of the woman who washes our clothes, and the man who carts off our rubbish, we shall find it easier to understand our neighbors, whether poor or rich.

But, in this world of past mistakes and present temptations, to do right requires also that we stop doing wrong. More and more clearly is the truth perceived, that in order that men may have freedom to live, they must have freedom of access to the source of life, — to the earth which the Lord hath given, not to certain favored individuals or classes, but to "the children of men." If the land of a nation belongs to the people of that nation, then there can hardly be a deeper underlying evil than the monopoly on the part of a few of the common heritage of all. It is that evil which we, in this new and apparently boundless country, are called to face. To remove the wrong of private property in land will not require any absurd attempt to reapportion the soil; but it will require the collection of the rental values of land, irrespective of improvements, as the fund from which the expenses of the city, State and nation shall be met. Until we make that change we are wronging every landless or unemployed or ill-paid person in the nation, and we shall be baffled in all our efforts to do them good.

Tolstoï says, " The present position which we, the educated and well-to-do classes, occupy is that of the Old Man of the Sea riding on the poor man's back, only, unlike the Old Man of the Sea, we are sorry for the poor man, very sorry. And we will do almost anything for the poor man's relief; we will not only supply him with food sufficient for him to keep on his legs, but we will provide him with cooling draughts concocted on strictly scientific principles; we will teach and instruct him and point out to him the beauties of the landscape; we will discourse sweet music to him and give him lots of good advice. Yes, we will do almost anything for the poor man, anything but get off his back."

The words are sharp, but are they any more searching than those of Henry Thoreau, from whom I just quoted? "If I devote myself," he says, "to other pursuit and contemplation" (than the simple common labor of every-day life), "I must first see, at least, that I do not pursue them sitting upon another man's shoulders. I must get off him first, that he may pursue his contemplation too."

Only let us remember that we are so involved with others in our political and economic life that we cannot free ourselves from the shame of this injustice, however we may see and detect it; we can only do our best to bring home the horror of it to other individuals, until the whole community is stung with the sense of its own misery, and, like Samson, breaks the bands that bind it down. That will not be a war of classes, but a struggle of the whole people to be free. And if we are to stir others to enlist in this campaign against the monopoly of the very earth and air and light, we must make all we do to meet the immediate wants of the needy or the suffering contribute to the propaganda of reform. We must still feed the hungry and clothe the naked, but we shall try to show them, if we can, whence hunger and nakedness proceed; we may open orphanages and shelters, but they will be training-schools for the new age; we may go down into the slums, but we shall remember the words of the dying Pestalozzi, "I lived like a beggar, that beggars might learn to live like men," and feel that our best mission is to show the poor how to make slums impossible.

In closing, it seems best to provide against possible misunderstanding by saying that in speaking of morality I have not meant merely a system of ethics or a code of manners. I have set forward morality as at once deeper and loftier than philanthropy, as furnishing philanthropy with its only foundation and its indispensable guide, because I believe that in order to bless the world we must first of all do the will of God. That aim covers the whole field of duty, for the service of God demands the whole man. I do not for a moment dream that we shall find a ground on which to resist legalized wrong, and the despotism of vested interests, until we have discovered that behind *laws* there is a changeless and righteous Law, and that even if the " highest crime be written in the highest law of the land," it may yet be known and branded as a crime, because there is in the souls of even plain and ordinary men the witness to an eternal Right.

Nor does it seem probable that in the future, any more than in the past, will men be able to recognize an absolute Law without an absolute Law-giver, or an eternal Right apart from an eternal Will, — not indeed a self-will, a will to live, but a sacrificial Will, a Will to love. And to speak out of my own experience, I do not find a sufficient safeguard against the taking of my own conceits for truth, and my own desires for right, or a sufficient support against selfishness and pride in my own heart, and a footing on which to bid other men resist those disturbing passions in themselves, save as I acknowledge that the unseen righteousness and love are manifested in a Word of God made flesh, in Jesus Christ, the Head of humanity, the Ruler of a visible and enduring Kingdom in which love and law are one.

And if the philanthropy that now calls us is a philanthropy that rests upon a recognition of universal relations among all men, I cannot think that it should refuse to declare to all men that the foundation of those relations is He Who in His One Person is very Man and very God, the centre of human society, because He is the presence in human society of Truth and Right and Love.

VI.

THE ETHICS OF SOCIAL PROGRESS.

By Professor Franklin H. Giddings, Bryn Mawr College.

He will teach "a blinding superstition," said Theophrastus Such, who teaches "that a theory of human well-being can be constructed in disregard of the influences that have made us human." If modern thought has any new truth to contribute to the inherited stock of ethical wisdom, it is because we are in a position to study more minutely than was possible in earlier days, and to interpret more exactly the forces and conditions by which our human nature has been wrought. We shall find them to be not altogether different in kind from those that were recognized by Plato, Aristotle, and Kant. Indeed, the Greek conceptions were truer than some later ones. Most of the ethical systems that have been constructed since the Protestant Reformation have dealt directly with the individual, and have attempted to work from the individual to society. In this they have been not wholly wrong. Centuries of suppression of individuality by Church and State had obscured one-half of moral truth. Men needed to be reminded that the individual, once he comes into existence, has a value in and for himself, and must be counted as a force reacting on society.

But to the extent that ethical systems have assumed the individual as an independent starting-point of social and moral phenomena, they have been radically untrue. The Greeks never failed to see that all rational life is a product of social conditions. To the Greek, says Butcher, "'The man *versus* the state' was a phrase unknown; the man was complete in the state; apart from it he was not only incomplete, he had no rational existence. Only through the social organism could each part, by adaptation to the others, develop its inherent powers."

Nevertheless, this doctrine of the creation of man by society was by no means completely thought out in the minds of those writers who first formulated it, and those who last concerned themselves about it left much to be added by the students of a later time. Aristotle's comparative study of one hundred and fifty-eight different communities, which enabled him first among scientific investigators to show in detail how and why the good life can have existence only in the organized state, was a theoretical no less than a practical advance beyond the speculative insight of Plato.

In like manner, our modern study of social progress is an advance, both theoretical and practical, beyond the work of Plato and Aristotle, and beyond the philosophy of man as it stood when post-Kantian idealism had achieved in Germany its task of reviving Hellenic moods of thought. The assertion demands, perhaps, a single word of explanation. They misapprehend the work of science who oppose it to speculative philosophy, as if one must choose between them which god he will serve.

It may be that our modern science can discover few great truths of which at least some glimmerings were not seen in ancient Greece. The very doctrine of evolution is in that sense not new. But the mission of science is a patient conversion of insight into sight ; of dialectic into knowledge. Our advantage is not in a surer conviction than Aristotle held, that he who can live without society must be either a beast or a god ; it is in a minute and relatively precise knowledge of those slow but certain processes of biological and social change by which the transformation of brutality into humanity is effected. And we cannot afford to despise this more perfect knowledge, as but a tedious elaboration of ideas long since familiar and accepted. It is itself a new factor in the social process.

In the fateful game of chess with the unseen antagonist of Mr. Huxley's picture, it enables man to play with the cool and calculating joy of one

who knows the meaning and the end of every
move ; knows, too, that on the other side the play,
though real and relentless, is always just, patient,
and fair.

Therefore, chief among the relations of cause
and effect in the wonderful process that has made
us human, is one that brings together, in a complete truth, the partial explanations that we owe
to Athens, with other explanations no less partial,
that have been worked out in our own day. The
action of a social medium upon intelligence and
character on the one hand, natural selection and
survival on the other, — these influences together
have created human faculty. There came a time
in the long struggle for existence, as Mr. Wallace
has shown, when mental resource counted for more
than physical strength. But anthropoid apes and
simian men, we have every reason to suppose, acquired mental resources through their social habits,
which multiplied experiences and made tradition
possible. The intelligence that association created
has never ceased to depend on association for per-
petuation and growth. Deprived of comradeship
by circumstance or law, men go back to the brutality from which they came. Wilfully rejecting
companionship they learn, with Manfred, that man
is not yet qualified to act the part of god:

> . . . "There is an order
> Of mortals on the earth, who do become
> Old in their youth, and die ere middle age,
> Without the violence of warlike death."

Therefore it has been the creatures best equipped with social habit and its products that have won and maintained supremacy in the ceaseless contention with physical nature and living enemies. Society is a means to a perfectly definite end, — namely, the survival of living creatures through a progressive evolution of their intelligence and sympathy. There can be no sociology worthy of the name which is not essentially an elaboration of this central principle. The notion that society is an end in itself amounts to an unthinkable proposition. At the same time, the intelligence and the fraternity that association creates, react in their turn on society, making it more perfect as a working organization, nobler and purer as a medium of individual life.

Thus the interpretation of man as a progressive ethical being, and the interpretation of society as an ever changing plexus of relationships, must proceed together. It is not enough to know with the philosophers of Greece that without society and social duty there can be no individual moral life. They understood well the problems of social order and the nature of personal worthiness. They knew that excellence is essentially a fact of organization: Plato's demonstration that justice in the state and goodness in the individual life are neither more nor less than the coordinated play of mutually dependent and mutually limiting activities, in proportions harmonious with

one another, and in perfect subordination to the
unity of the whole, has never been equalled, certainly never surpassed, in ethical analysis. They
were familiar, too, with a thousand aspects of social
and of individual change.

But they did not combine these elements into
a synthetic conception. They were unable to
unite the static with the dynamic factors of
their problem, and so arrive at the peculiarly
modern notion of a moving equilibrium. And,
therefore, they failed to achieve an entirely true
and sufficient philosophy of either man or the
state. For life is not the whirl of a constant
number of jugglers' plates, balanced on the sword-
points of the players: it is a whirl in which
new plates and new motions appear at every
instant, compelling ever most delicate readjust-
ments throughout the entire system, and yet without once disturbing seriously the approximately
perfect balance of the whole. The large and difficult conception, then, to which we must attain, is
that of a world in which there can be no true ethical phenomena except through a process, at once
progressive and orderly, of mutual modifications
and adaptations of man and society by each other;
in which each acquires, stage by stage, a more delicate complexity of organization. Of the many
implications of this conception we must now examine some of the more important.

In philosophy of every school the term personality

stands for the highest synthetic product of mental evolution. True personality is a well-unified, self-conscious mental life, harmonious within itself, capable of indefinite expansion, and sympathetic with surrounding life because realizing and comprehending in itself the manifold possibilities of life. It is the type at once of the concrete and the universal. One who thoroughly understands this will never make the mistake of believing, on the one hand, that utility is the fundamental word of ethics, or, on the other hand, that ethics can be complete without including utilitarianism.

The fundamental word of ethics is integrity, — wholeness. There can be no utility apart from a consciousness capable of wants and satisfactions. The integrity, the unity, the internal harmony of that consciousness is therefore the first necessity. The strongest ethical terms, as right, truth, obligation, stand in direct relation to integrity rather than to utility. The joy of activity also, including the supreme satisfaction that one may find in self-sacrifice, is related to integrity first of all, for it implies the consistent action of the whole personality; while utility is a quality, not immediately of conduct as spontaneous activity, but rather of its reactions.

Therefore if integrity and utility come into direct conflict, utility must for the moment give way; since self-conservation is preliminary to self-ex-

pansion; and because the vitality and the qualities
of conduct, by which all its own consequences are
conditioned, are governed by its internal unity of
purpose. But there can be no enduring integrity
without development, no permanent conservation
without progress. Therefore ethics cannot stop at
integrity. It must expand into utilitarianism, and
work out the laws of that cumulative happiness
which is the reward and the confirmation of well-
doing.

Put this conception of personality side by side
with our view of intelligence as a product of social
conditions. Is it not evident that personality in
this philosophical sense comes into being only in
the relatively perfect society, which has passed
beyond the limitations of tribal existence, and
even of a narrow nationalism, into a sympathetic
relation to mankind in all its varied phases of
development? If so, it is a product of progressive
as distinguished from both stationary and anar-
chistic, or disintegrating, society, and the theory of
personality can be worked out only in terms of a
theory of social progress.

In detail this means that a society in which the
highest type of mind can appear is one that has
had, first, such a vigorous ethnical or national
existence, and second, such varied contact with
surrounding peoples, that it has become plastic
without losing its distinctive character. In the
nomenclature of evolution it has acquired internal

mobility without losing cohesion. By admixture of bloods a variable but not unstable physical nature has been produced. By numberless comparisons of one mode of civilization with another, a mental temper at once critical and catholic has been created. Prosperity and a rapidly increasing population have constantly brought the young and enterprising to the front in the conduct of affairs. Selection has weeded out those who could neither learn nor forget. Force and authority in the social organization have so far given way to spontaneous initiative that the individual can find scope for the development of his latent powers, but not so far as to permit disintegration. Contact and converse being the conditions of progress, its phases are an increase of material well-being, an inclusive sympathy, a catholic rationality, and a flexible social constitution, adapting itself readily to changing conditions, yet of enduring strength. And since the conservation of energy is a fact of social as of physical phenomena, the essential nature of progress, beneath all conditions and phases, is a conversion of lower, that is more simple, imperfectly organized, modes of energy into higher. Economic activities transform the energies of physical nature into social force, of which there is no other source whatever, since artistic, religious, educational, and political activities are but a further transformation of the results of economic effort. In the medium of all these activities is moulded their final product, the human personality, which could come into being in no other way and under no other circumstances.

Such are a few of the sociological facts that underlie ethical problems. It is interesting to reflect that in a vague way the great truth which they contain, that without social progress there can be no human personality, and, therefore, no ethics, has always been present in popular consciousness. The experiences of individual life, of course, afford a basis for it, since the years from childhood to maturity are normally a period of increasing personal power, in which every ambitious man believes that he was born to accomplish some desirable transformation of the community.

But social experiences in the mass have doubtless built the superstructure. Studies in ethnology and comparative religions are pointing to the probable conclusion that faith in progress has been an essential element in every religious belief. Under some circumstances it may be the only element. Charity-workers in the slums of Paris and London report that an undefined, shadowy belief in a better state of things is the last trace of religious consciousness discoverable in whole classes of the very poor. What has been the genesis of the conviction? Everywhere social advance has been brought about through successive waves of conquest. Naturally enough, in the minds of the conquerors the good order, the right order, has been identified with the new order of things which they have sought to establish. The evil order has been the old way of life that was followed by the subjugated enemies who are now reduced to serfdom. Good spirits are those who favor the plans of the enterprising and successful, in whose control are the shaping of public policy and the dictation of orthodox belief. It is true that orthodoxy is no sooner born than it turns conservative, and seeks to maintain itself against further change. But the effort is vain. Another conquest, or a new generation, brings new men and new issues to the fore, and a new orthodoxy stands ever ready to crowd the old relentlessly to the wall. The conquered and oppressed, on their part, have a doctrine of progress also. It is a faith in a future in which justice shall be done, when they shall be delivered from their captivity, and in their turn put their ruthless enemies under foot. In time a closer intercourse and a finer feeling soften and blend these conflicting faiths into a belief in the ultimate happiness and perfection of all classes.

Crude and even visionary as it may be, this perennial faith in social progress is the motive power of moral life. Science must rectify it at a thousand points ; but the very first word of an ethical science that is not charlatanism itself must be an unequivocal declaration that such faith *in se* is the beginning of righteousness. The first law of life is a law of motion. In society, as on the street, the

preliminary duty is to "move on." The nation
that has no further reconstructions to effect, no
new ideals to realize in practice, has completed its
work and will disappear before the warfare or the
migrations of more earnest men. But the moving
on must be developmental; mere change is not
evolution but confusion; and the nature and limitations of an evolutionary process, imperfectly recognized as yet in ethical discussion, are practically
unknown to popular thought. It is here, then,
that the rectifying work of science must begin.

Human society is not a something-for-nothing
endowment order. The vision of a completed society, lacking neither material comfort nor any moral
excellence, in which foolishness, want, and suffering could linger only as dim memories of an imperfect past, has had a strangely persistent fascination
for speculative minds in every age. Common sense
has never accepted the dream for reality; for common sense is a sceptic from the beginning. Philosophy has doubted if evil be not inherent in the
nature of the world, and therefore ineradicable.
But doubt and scepticism have fallen far short of
reasoned demonstration from experience that the
vision is inherently absurd.

Yet the elements of the demonstration that
science has been patiently working out in recent
years are simple enough. The available energy
of society at any given moment is strictly limited in amount. The total can be increased only

by parting with some, in the thought and labor by which larger stores of physical energy, contained in the natural resources of the environment, are set free and converted to human use. All progress, therefore, is conditioned by cost, and if the law of conservation holds good in these matters, as we have assumed that it must, the cost will increase with the progress ; not, however, necessarily in the same ratio as the gain, since riper knowledge should enable us to get more from physical nature with a given expenditure of human effort. In this simple form the limitations of progress present an economic rather than a moral problem, and need not detain us at the present time.

But since society is an organic aggregate, the cost of progress takes on various complications, out of which grow ethical problems that are both grave and difficult. As was shown in the illustration of the moving equilibrium, society, as an aggregate that is simultaneously losing and absorbing motion, must experience an incessant rearrangement of its parts. This means two very important things: First, there can be no social gain that does not entail somewhere, on the whole community or on a class, the break-up of long-established relations, interests, and occupations, and the necessity of a more or less difficult readjustment. Second, the increase of social activity, which is the only phase of progress that most people ever see at all, may so exceed the rate of constructive readjustment that the end is disorganization and ruin.

For the further examination of these propositions let us translate them from physical terms into the language of feeling. This is legitimate, because the destruction of familiar relations and the necessity of establishing new ones are known immediately in consciousness in terms of hardship or suffering; while any disorganization of social or individual life involves the pain of moral retrogression. The limitations of progress then are these: First, there can be no social progress, and therefore no evolution of ethical personality, except at the price of an absolute, but not necessarily a relative, increase of suffering. Second, if the increase of social activity, which is one phase of progress, becomes disproportionate to the constructive reorganization of social relationships, which is the complementary phase, the increase of suffering will become degeneration and moral evil.

Such limitations are not a cheering aspect of social progress, but their reality is fully established in historical and statistical fact, and they sharply define our ethical obligations. The first of these sobering propositions has to be made a shade darker still. The suffering that progress costs is borne for the most part vicariously. The classes who are displaced, whose interests and occupations are broken up by the relentless course of change, are not the ones who secure the joys of richer and ampler life. That which enormously benefits mankind is too often the irretrievable ruin of the few. For illustration, one need not be confined to the familiar facts of the wasting of barbarian peoples before the advance of civilization, or the sacrifice of life in national self-defence. The history of industrial progress affords examples quite as striking and essentially more significant, since they show that after society has settled down to the quiet occupations of peace, the fundamental conditions of its development remain unchanged. In reviewing them the sociologist expects to find that the minority which thus suffers the pains of progress is composed mainly of the most unprogressive elements of the population, and he is not disappointed. But he finds evidences also that to some extent the sufferers are recruited by victims of pure misfortune; neither their nature nor their conduct has been the cause of their undoing.

When in the thirteenth and fourteenth centuries the growth of towns, money payments, and the commutation of week work loosened the bonds of custom and law that had held the serf to the manor, the entire commonwealth of England experienced an economic prosperity never before known. Population and wealth increased, and the free tenants, as a class, rose steadily in social position. They could cultivate more or less land, or engage in trade and obtain municipal charters.

But the economic equality of an earlier day had dis-
appeared. The growth of population brought men
into the world for whom there were places enough,
and more than enough, but not places already
allotted to them in the social order. They were
places that had to be discovered by intelligence
and enterprise, qualities that are not possessed
by all men equally. The full virgate of land
was no longer secured by customary law to each
family. Since the energetic and strong could control more, the easy-going and weak had to get on
with less. In the towns the far-seeing and fore-
handed quickly monopolized trade and the more
profitable crafts. And so, while this comparative
freedom of enterprise stimulated activity in a hundred ways that made England as a nation richer
and stronger, it destroyed the old economic footing of the less competent members of society, and
left them to struggle on, thenceforth, as a wage-
earning class.

Two hundred years later, in the sixteenth century, society was again transformed by the results
of geographical discovery. Free capital and foreign
commerce quickened industry and thought into
intense and brilliant life. "It was indeed a stirring time," writes Hyndman, obliged to admit that
this period, which he calls the iron age of the
peasantry and wage classes, was, nevertheless, one
of marvellous progress in other respects. "A new
world was being discovered in art and in science

in Europe as well as in actual existence on the other side of the Atlantic. . . . Never before had so great an impulse been given to human enterprise and human imagination." But the splendor had its price, a price that socialists like Hyndman have superficially described and most imperfectly understood. Political integration had been going on. The struggle of contending factions had been costly, and the re-established national life, with its manifold activities, was more costly. Barons discharged the bands of retainers that were no longer needed in civil strife. To better their fortunes they enclosed common lands that had been freely used by the yeomanry, and began evicting tenants to convert agricultural lands into the sheep pastures that required little labor and returned a quick money income from sales of wool in Flanders.

Now the misery of these displaced people, forced into wage labor and vagabondage, was not due to any actual lack of land or of industrial opportunity. There remained land enough and to spare, notwithstanding enclosures and evictions, had it been used rightly; the development of manufactures and commerce had only begun. If they had had the knowledge and will to cultivate arable land more intensively they could not have been driven from the soil; if there had been a free mobility of labor they could have found employment quickly in the best instead of tardily in the worst markets, as too often happened; if the organizing ability of em-

ployers had been greater the best markets would
more quickly have found them.

But the social value of land had become too
great for their wasteful methods; they had to
change or go. That knowledge might increase;
that freedom to go and come might be established;
that the organization of enterprise might become
more perfect, it was necessary that just these economic and social changes which accomplished so
much ruin should take place. Consequently, if
the world was to become a larger and better place
for the alert, on-moving many, the sacrifice of the
sluggish had to be.

The industrial revolution at the close of the
eighteenth century occasioned displacements of
labor that bore more distinctly the character of
misfortunes to those who were injured by them.
No degree of skill, enterprise, or assiduity, could
have enabled the handicraftsmen to hold their own
in competition with power-machinery and the
steam-engine. They could do nothing but leave
their shops to wind and weather, and begin life
over, on new terms, in factory towns. How many
thousands of them never fully re-established themselves, how many succumbed to illness or even to
actual starvation before economic reorganization
was fairly completed, the reports of parliamentary
inquiries bear witness.

Yet an unprecedented increase of population
was proof that, on the whole, the masses of the

people had never been so prosperous. Before
1751 the largest decennial increase had been
three per cent; before 1781 it did not exceed
six per cent. Then, all at once, it rose, decade by
decade, to nine, eleven, fourteen, and finally, between 1811 and 1821, to eighteen per cent. At
the present time the displacement of manual labor
by machinery is incessant, and less than in any
previous period is the suffering visited on the least
valuable portion of the population, since not in-
frequently it is men of a higher standard of life
who are forced out by the competition of a lower
type. Nevertheless, so enormous has been the
net gain from improved methods of production that
the consequences of displacement are immeasurably
less serious than they were a century ago. The
chances of finding re-employment quickly are, for
competent men, far greater than they were at any
former time, and the period of search is made en-
durable by accumulated savings and varied forms
of aid. All in all, industrial history discloses a
progressive diminution of the proportion of inevitable suffering mixed with the gains of progress.
But the absolute increase remains. The personnel
of the displaced class changes more rapidly than in
earlier times, but the class, as a class, is endlessly
renewed. As a class, it can never disappear so long
as progress continues.

Such, in its simplest statement, is the law of the
cost of progress. " He that increaseth knowledge

increaseth sorrow." Whatever augments well-
being destroys some livelihood. As an abstract
proposition no well-informed student of social
phenomena would call this truth in question.
But, unfortunately, the law-makers, the social re-
formers, and the moralists have not bound it upon
their fingers nor written it upon the tables of their
hearts. They legislate, reform, and advise, for-
getful that their wisest endeavors can be at the
best only "something between a hinderance and a
help"; and the world goes on, therefore, not only
deceiving itself with dreams, but wasting its resources on impossible undertakings.

For this principle is one that would make the
instant quietus of many vain questionings if it
were an ever-present element in our thinking.
The poor have been always with us. Must they
be with us always? Or may we hope that economic prosperity and social justice will one day
mete out comfort, if not abundance, to all? Not
unless we can attain "finality in a world of
change." Not unless there is a definite limit to
the intellectual and moral progress of the race,
for the conditions that would eliminate poverty
from the earth would infallibly terminate the life
that is more than meat, in society first, and afterwards in individuals. Unless all men could be
made equally prudent, equally judicious, neither
an increase of wealth nor changes in its distribution could prevent the occasional sweeping away

of possessions by the social rearrangements that progress demands. The relative dimensions of poverty will contract and its misery will be alleviated, but there is no reason to believe that it will ever wholly disappear.

Will multitudes of human beings remain always in practical subjection to individual or corporate masters? Can we not abolish economic slavery as we have abolished legal bondage? Aristotle's argument that slavery inheres in civilization has shocked the sensitive and amused the shallow, while both have quoted it to show what foolishness a philosopher can teach. But to the wise it will ever remain a profound though mournful truth.

Essential slavery has been aptly described as the estate of a man who " can't get any freedom." We have changed the legal conditions under which millions of men and women perform ill-requited tasks of daily toil. To some extent we have diminished the total magnitude of their misery, if not in every individual case its extreme intensity. But we have not enabled them to get actual freedom. We have made it unlawful to buy and sell their persons. The master can no longer obtain control of the laborer's time and strength, and therefore of his freedom, from any legal principal but the laborer himself. The laborer cannot even sell his own freedom in perpetuity. But he can sell any portion of it, or all of it subdivided into portions, for a limited period of time, or for his whole life subdivided into periods.

Practically, therefore, any man or woman may sell his or her entire freedom for life, and practically thousands of both men and women are compelled by hunger to make the sale on terms that are personally degrading. Yet that interpretation of this melancholy fact which attributes it to the wickedness and greed of a capital-owning class is a tissue of economic and sociological fallacies. Another interpretation, which explains it as unavoidable misfortune, becomes a perversion of history when, in the desire to prove that the world has grown better, it assumes that ancient legal slavery was a consciously-devised oppression. Neither oppression nor greed has been at any time the first cause of legal bondage or of economic dependence. Both are secondary causes, induced by experiences with a slavery already existent.

Modern civilization does not require, it does not even need, the drudgery of needle-women or the crushing toil of men in a score of life-destroying occupations. If these wretched beings should drop out of existence and no others stood ready to fill their places, the economic activities of the world would not greatly suffer. A thousand devices latent in inventive brains would quickly make good any momentary loss. The true view of the facts is that these people continue to exist after the kinds of work that they know how to perform have ceased to be of any considerable value to society. Society continues to employ them for a remuneration not exceeding the cost of getting the work done in some other and perhaps better way.

The economic law here referred to is one that has been too much neglected in scientific discussion. It ought to be repeated and illustrated at every opportunity, for at present it stands in direct contradiction to current prepossessions. We are told incessantly that unskilled labor creates the wealth of the world. It would be nearer the truth to say that large classes of unskilled labor hardly create their own subsistence. The laborers that have no adaptiveness, that bring no new ideas to their work, that have no suspicion of the next best thing to turn to in an emergency, might be much better identified with the dependent classes than with the wealth-creators. Precisely the same economic law offers the true interpretation of ancient slavery. In strictness civilization did not rest on slavery. It was not in any true sense maintained by slavery. The conditions that created the civilization created economic dependence, and they are working in the same way, with similar results, to-day.

Ancient civilization accepted the dependence and utilized it in the crude form of slavery. Modern civilization accepts and utilizes it in the slightly more refined form of the wages system.

Certain great social tasks of creative organization
have always confronted our race. The enforced
effort to achieve them has been history's great
competitive examination. The slaves and serfs
have been those who have failed. The first great
necessity was social unity, — the power to act together in a disciplined way, — and the first slaves
were those who could not create a sufficiently
coherent social organization to sustain a growing
civilization. They had to make way before others
who were equal to that great achievement, and
they became slaves not solely nor chiefly because
of a conqueror's tyranny, but primarily because
slavery or serfdom was practically the only economic disposition that could be made of them.
To-day social unity has been in good measure
established, and the world has entered on yet
larger undertakings. The condition and assurance
of freedom to-day is the ability to devise new
things, to create new opportunities, to make not
only two blades of grass grow where one grew
before, but to make a hundred kinds of grass grow
where before grew only one kind.

Accordingly, the practically unfree task-workers
of this present time are those who, unaided, can
accomplish none of these new things. They are
those who might do well in old familiar ways, but
who have nothing to turn to when their ways cease
to be of value to the world. To live they must
force depreciated services upon society on any

terms that society can continue to pay. They are unfree task-workers not because society chooses to oppress them, but because society has not yet devised or stumbled upon any other disposition to make of them. Civilization, therefore, is not cruel. It is ever supporting and trying in many ways to utilize the wrecks and failures of its own imperfect past.

But it may be said: All these negative conclusions are based on the assumption that the *régime* of individualism is to continue. Might not redemption from poverty and dependence be possible under the reign of a beneficent socialism?

Two systems of socialism have been proposed, if we classify them according to plans of organization, and two if we classify with reference to a proposed division of wealth. According to one plan industrial administration would be centralized; according to the other it would be decentralized. Either of these systems might be communistic, incomes being made equal throughout society, or either might be non-communistic, the services of different men being valued unequally.

Decentralized socialism would merely substitute competing communities for competing private organizations. It would follow that some communities would prosper more than others, and that some, therefore, would presently come under subjection to the others. A centralized socialism would probably attempt to establish a rigid and

final system of occupations, in the hope of pre-
venting industrial derangements. If successful
the attempt would make an end of progress. If
no such attempt were made, men would be thrown,
as now, from time to time, out of that ideal arrangement in which each did the work to which he was
best adapted, and therefore, if rewarded in proportion to their services, the unfortunates would
receive, as now, only the pittance that would
barely support life. The one difference would be
that society in its corporate capacity would assume
the responsibility of finding new work for them;
but, rewarding them according to performance
only, it would practically have them in absolute
subjection. They would only have exchanged
masters, and slavery to individuals for slavery to
society.

If, vainly hoping to escape from this dilemma,
society should not only assume the responsibility
of finding new opportunities for the displaced, but
should undertake to compensate them for the
buffetings and losses that they had suffered by
reason of industrial changes, and regardless of
their resulting worth to the commonwealth, it
would radically transform the character of its
socialism. Rewarding no longer according to service, the socialism would become communism.
Men of unequal power to work and to use, of
widely varying capacities to enjoy, would share
alike the common product of their labor. Only

one result could follow. Men of animal natures, having as large incomes as men of a higher mental and moral development, would spend inevitably a disproportionate share on the grosser sorts of gratification. Materialism of life, with all its moral debasement, would be the unprofitable substitute for economic hardship. Income can never be greatly disproportionate to the social value of a man's work, talents, culture and virtues, without degrading him. If it be said that at present many men whose whole social value is of the slightest, do have, in fact, fabulous incomes, which socialism would diminish, the reply is that there are not, accurately speaking, many such men, and that there would be no apparent advantage in substituting a systematic breeding of dull sensualists for the sporadic genesis of more brilliant debauchees. Be that as it may, the men and women of this class exemplify and verify the law. Their lives lend the sting of truth to the saying, "How hardly shall they that have riches enter into the kingdom of God."

Shall we then conclude that an unrestrained individualism, eagerly working out those social changes that seem advantageous to their promoters, can achieve limitless progress, and that only harm could come from any checking of the rate or intensity of its activity? Shall we assume that the inevitable costs of progress in economic loss and human suffering must be uncomplainingly borne by those on whom they fall, because all private reforms are utopian, and all public regulation of industry or assumption of its losses in accordance with any form of socialism or communism would be worse than folly? Must we acknowledge that society has no moral responsibility for the consequences of the processes and changes by which its own well-being and ethical life are maintained? Shall we give ourselves over to the belief that *laissez faire* is the last word of social science and the first law of ethics? Assuredly and most emphatically, no! Nothing in the conditions of progress as set forth in the foregoing study so much as hints at other than negative answers to these questions. On the contrary, if the law of evolution as exemplified in human society has been rightly understood, we shall be prepared to find certain very real limitations of the number and extent of the social, political, or industrial metamorphoses which, within a given period, can combine in genuine progress. We shall look to discover a growing necessity for integral social action. We shall expect to hear the ethical consciousness of humanity declaring that society is morally responsible for the costs of its existence.

In dynamic phenomena of every kind results are a function, as the mathematicians express it, of time. With a given amount of energy you can go in an hour or a day a given distance. Prolong the time and you can increase the distance. In

the inconceivably complicated dynamic phenomena
of life, — growth, organization, development are
all functions of time. Force the rate of transformation and you simply prevent the establishment
of some relations of integration, differentiation, or
segregation, necessary to complete organization.
And if organization is incomplete there is a limit
to the life-possibilities of the organism. It can
perform less and enjoy less while it lives, and its
dissolution will begin earlier. Society on a great
scale, as the individual life on a smaller scale, ex-
emplifies all these laws. If social evolution is to
continue, and the ethical life of man is to become
larger and richer with increasing happiness, social
organization in the future will be not simpler than
it is now, but immeasurably more complex. In
its larger being individualism, socialism, and communism will not be the mutually exclusive things
that they now seem to be. There will be not a
narrower but a wider field for individual effort,
not less but more personal liberty. At the same
time, more enterprises will be brought under public control, and more of the good things of life
will be distributed, like the sunshine and the air,
in free and equal portions. The displaced men
and women will be more quickly re-established
than now, their services will be made of greater
value, and society will assume a larger portion of
the burden of their misfortunes. All these things
are implications of the second of the limitations of

progress to which attention has been called, —
namely, that if the increase of social activity becomes disproportionate to the constructive reorganization of social relationships, the increase of
suffering will become degeneration and moral
evil. Some of the facts in evidence must be
briefly noted.

Dazzled by the magnificent results of material
progress already achieved, men throw themselves
into the great enterprises of modern life with the
zest of an ambition that knows no bounds. The
rate of industrial, professional, political, and intellectual activity becomes proportionate to the swift-
ness of electricity and steam. The intense struggle
for success causes three great demographic changes
which profoundly modify the social conditions of
existence.

The first is a phenomenal increase of population,
following an enormous production of wealth. We
have already seen how improved industrial conditions in England, in the first part of this century,
were followed instantly by an unprecedented increase of population. At the present time the
increase of population in England and Wales by
births in excess of deaths is not less than one
thousand souls daily. The expansion of the population of the United States from 3,929,214 in 1790
to 62,622,250 in 1890, while the population of
Europe, in spite of enormous emigration, has been
rapidly multiplying, is a phenomenon that Long-

staff accurately describes as absolutely unique in history.

The second change referred to is a rapid concentration of this increasing population in large cities, where the great prizes of worldly success are striven for and won. This movement and its consequences are already attracting the serious attention of sociologists to the grave problems they present. Of the 1000 daily births in access of deaths in England and Wales, 408 are born in the seventy-six largest cities and towns, 592 in the country, but only 437 remain in the country-places of their birth; 112 migrate to the cities, and 43 to foreign lands. In the United States in 1790 3.35 per cent of the population lived in cities of 8000 or more inhabitants. Now 29.12 per cent live in cities of equal or larger size, while in the Atlantic coast division, comprising the New England States, New York, New Jersey, Pennsylvania, and Maryland, more than one-half of the population are urban inhabitants. This means that population is flowing into the cities much faster than the reorganization of the manifold phases of town life, including municipal government, is making urban conditions as wholesome as those of the country. The result is that constant drain upon the fresh vitality of the country to meet the incessant destruction of vitality in the towns which makes the depopulation of rural sections so grave a matter for the future of civilization. " By a curious perversion," says Longstaff, "the advantage of towns is said to be 'life.' There is in truth more life in a given space, more high pressure, more rush; but it is the rush of a clock running down."

A displacement, in certain industries, of men of a relatively high standard of life by cheaper men of a lower standard, more rapidly than the better men can find places in industries requiring relatively intelligent labor, is the third demographic consequence of intense activity. The normal displacement, as has been shown, is of the dull, mechanical, non-adaptable man by a more versatile competitor. But industries are not all of the same character. Some are more progressive in their methods than others because they contribute to the satisfaction of constantly developing wants, which create a varying demand, while others minister to wants that are relatively stationary. In some, therefore, the high-priced man is the cheap man; in others the low-priced man is the cheaper man.

Economists who have contended that high wages mean a low cost of labor, and those who have affirmed the contrary are alike half right and half wrong. They have been observing different classes of industries. Under a perfectly uniform, self-regulating circulation of labor, the versatile man, of the high standard of life, would displace the cheaper man in one class of industries, and the duller, cheaper man would displace higher-priced labor in the other class. Under normal progress the major displacement would be of inferior by superior men.

But unless economic evolution, creating new wants and varying demands, and reorganizing industry to supply them, is going on more rapidly than the growth of social unrest, or of those political policies that so often force vast hordes of destitute people into migrations that have no definite destination, as in the case of the Russian Jews, there may be a cruel and ruinous substitution of the lower for the higher grade of workmen, prematurely and far beyond normal limits. It would not be unfortunate that the Irishman should displace the native American, that the French Canadian should in turn displace the Irishman, and that finally the Hungarian or the Pole should displace the French Canadian, if the men of the higher standard of life could immediately step into industries of a higher grade. But when this is not possible, when they can live only by sinking to the level of their more brutal competitors, it is an evil of great magnitude.

Under such circumstances the intense competition of the struggle for success, due partly to ambition, but primarily to the quickening rate of industrial and social transformation, piles up in the community a frightful wreckage of physical and moral degeneration. Every sociologist, every statistician, has been struck with the seemingly

anomalous fact that suicide, insanity, crime, vagabondage, increase with wealth, education, and 'refinement; that they are, in a word, as Morselli
says, phenomena of civilization. But the fact is
not altogether anomalous, after all. These things
are a part of the cost of progress, forms that the
cost of progress takes when the rate of social
activity exceeds the rate of constructive reorganization. Quicken the pace of a moving army, and
the number of the unfortunates who will fall ex-
hausted by the way will be disproportionately
increased. Besides quickening the pace, let discipline lapse and organization break up, and the
number of stragglers will be more than doubled.
Increase the strain of any kind of competitive work
and derange the conditions under which it is done,
and the percentage of failures will rise. That
this is the far-reaching explanation of the physical,
intellectual, and moral degeneration that we behold
on every side, notwithstanding a marvellous multiplication of all the influences that make for good,
is not to be doubted by one who will patiently
study the facts recorded in moral and vital statistics. Thus, the number of suicides in Italy was
29 per 1,000,000 inhabitants in 1864, when her
people were just entering on a new and larger life
under national unity. In 1877 it had risen to 40
per 1,000,000. In France, in 1827, the number
was 48 per 1,000,000. Before 1875 it had risen
to 155. In England a rate of 62 in 1830 had

risen to 73 in 1876. In Saxony a rate of 158 in 1836 had risen to 391 in 1877.[1] Is it any wonder that Morselli, from whose laborious monograph these figures are taken, says that "in the aggregate of the civilized States of Europe and America the frequency of suicide shows a growing and uniform increase, so that generally voluntary death since the beginning of the century has increased and goes on increasing more rapidly than the geometrical augmentation of the population and of the general mortality?" Elsewhere he says, and his figures prove, that "it is those countries which possess a higher standard of general culture which furnish the largest contingent of voluntary deaths," and that the proportion of suicides is greater in the condensed population of urban centres than among the more scattered inhabitants of the country.

The phenomena of insanity follow the same general laws, with the difference that the abnormal loneliness of isolated country districts, drained of their population and social resources by migration to the cities, is as deleterious as the

[1] Later figures, given by Maurice Block ("L'Europe Politique et Sociale," deuxième édition, 1893, p. 460) are as follows: Italy, 1888, 53 per 1,000,000 inhabitants, 1889, 47 per 1,000,000; France, 1889, 212 per 1,000,000; England, 1889, 80 per 1,000,000. In Massachusetts the proportion was 69 per 1,000,000 in the period 1851–55 and 90.9 in the period 1881–85. *Vide* "Statistics of Suicide in New England," by Davis R. Dewey, *Publications of the American Statistical Association*, June–September, 1892.

overcrowding and fierce competition of towns. According to the figures of the Eleventh Federal Census the inmates of public asylums and hospitals for the insane are 2.10 per 1000 inhabitants in the North Atlantic division and 2.25 per 1000 in the Western division. It is in these sections that life is most intense. In the North Central division the ratio is 1.28 to 1000, in the South Atlantic division the ratio is 1.27 to 1000, and in the South Central division it is only 0.71 to 1000. Some allowance must be made for the larger number of deranged persons not committed to public institutions in some sections than in others, but this will not greatly affect the interpretation of the figures, an interpretation fully borne out by the researches of specialists. Maudsley, for example, says, "I cannot but think that the extreme passion for getting rich, absorbing the whole energies of life, predisposes to mental degeneracy in offspring, either to moral defect or to intellectual deficiency, or to outbursts of positive insanity."

That crime is an effect of poverty it is no longer possible to believe, since it varies independently of poverty, and directly with other social conditions and with the strain of progress. Thus, serious crimes, including theft, are not more frequent in poor than in wealthy countries. On the contrary, in England the trials for theft are 228 per 100,000 inhabitants, annually, while in Ireland they are but 101, in Hungary 82, and in Spain 74.

Everywhere, too, crimes are less frequent in winter, when the hardships of poverty are most grievous, than in summer when they are more easily borne. Again, crime is not a monopoly of the poor, since all classes contribute to our jail and prison population in very nearly exact proportion to their total numbers, and Professor Falkner has shown that in the United States serious crime is more frequently committed by the native than by the foreign-born.

On the other hand, keener competition is everywhere followed by increasing criminality, as is most strikingly shown by the statistics of criminality among women. The crimes of women have been heretofore in small proportion to the crimes of men; but with the opening of hundreds of new industrial and professional opportunities to the sex hitherto shielded from the fiercer contentions of the social life-struggle, the figures of arrests and commitments of women show a sad increase. "In all countries where social habits and customs constrain women to lead retiring and secluded lives," says Morrison, "the number of female criminals descends to a minimum." In Greece, in 1889, there were only 50 women in a total prison population of 5023. In England, on the other hand, women constitute 17 per cent of the whole number of offenders, while in Scotland, where the industrial emancipation of women is most complete, no less than 27 per cent of the offences tried in criminal courts in 1880 were committed by women, and in 1888 that percentage had risen to 37.

Of the rapid increase of vagabondage, with social unrest and industrial evolution, but a word need be said. Professor McCook, of Trinity College, Hartford, who has made an exhaustive study of this question, finds that we are supporting in this country an army of 48,848 tramps. At the lowest estimate it costs to feed these absolutely worthless wretches $7,938,520 a year. Adding their hospital, jail, and prison expenses, the total becomes $9,000,000.

The end of these things would be social disintegration and paralysis but for a reaction that they start in the public mind. The ethical consciousness of society is aroused and unified by such evidences that civilization and progress are not an unmixed good. The demand becomes daily more imperative for a public and private philanthropy that shall be governed by the results of scientific inquiry; which shall work no longer at cross purposes, but merge their plans and efforts in a unified policy to ameliorate, so far as possible, conditions that man can never wholly remove, but which he can easily make worse. How far can the demand be met?

The practical solution of the problem depends on a difficult combination of two very difficult things. The first is to convince one set of people that society ought to assume the costs of its progress, and, so far as possible, take openly the responsibility for replacing the displaced. This is the element of truth in socialism. We have, indeed, made some progress in this direction. Practically and theoretically society admitted the obligation when, in the reigns of the Tudors, it began to supplement private and ecclesiastical charity by systems of public relief. In a hundred forms of legislation and administration, in public education, in the multiplication of asylums and hospitals, in a thousand modes of private beneficence, the duty is being more adequately discharged by each later generation. But we are yet very far from comprehending its full extent. We realize but faintly how far the incompetent and impoverished have been made such by social movements that have cut them off from any possibility of personal improvement. The second difficulty is to convince another set of people of the fallacy of a cardinal socialistic notion, — namely, that industrial derangements can be prevented in a progressive world; to convince them, therefore, that at all times a portion of mankind must be relatively useless to the community, and, for that reason, relatively poor; and that their greatest possible utilization and compensation depend on their being held for the while in practical subjection to other individuals or to the commonwealth.

We have heard a great deal in recent years about Christian socialism, and one of the most interesting

developments in the ecclesiastical world is the growing belief that Christianity ought to prove its pre-
tensions by demonstrating its power to solve social
problems. It is curious that in all this discussion
the most important single doctrine that Christianity has to contribute to social science has been forgotten or ignored. The doctrine referred to is that
of the distinction between those who are free from
the law and those who are under bondage to the
law. The key to the solution of the social problem
will be found in a frank acceptance of the fact
that one portion of every community is inherently
progressive, resourceful, creative, capable of self-
mastery and self-direction, while another portion,
capable of none of these things, can be made useful, comfortable, and essentially free, only by being
brought under bondage to society and kept under
mastership and discipline until they have acquired
power to help and govern themselves. If one
should say that we all believe this doctrine, — that
it is in no sense new, — the necessary reply would
be that we, nevertheless, habitually disregard it in
every matter save the juridical distinction between
the law-abiding and the criminal. We accept *laissez faire* as the expedient rule for all men and all
industries alike, or we denounce it as bad for all
alike. We advocate socialistic methods for the
entire field of industry, or we pronounce them im-
practicable for any part of it. We denounce compulsory education for any class in the community,

or we insist on forcing it on all classes. In all which sayings and doings we confound unlike things, and show ourselves irrational in the last degree.

What, then, in concrete detail, are some of the ethical obligations placed upon individuals and upon society by the conditions of social progress?

The law that the progressive, self-governing members of society should lay on themselves must include at least three groups of duties. First, they must resist, personally and in their influence, the tendency to subordinate every higher consideration to that mere quickening of competitive activity which so easily goes beyond its normal function of means to end, to become an irrational, unjustifiable end in itself. Especially in the education of children who are seen to be ambitious, should everything that savors of competition be absolutely put away. The competitive examination of such children is nothing less than essential crime, essential insanity, essential idiocy, for all these things will be among its results. Second, they must resort more freely, as fortunately they are beginning to do, to country-life, and especially must they provide the conditions of country-life to the greatest possible extent for children, not only their own but those of the city poor. Third, they must cultivate that true individuality in the consumption of wealth, which is not only the mark of genuine manliness or womanliness, but which surely acts on economic demand in ways that give a competitive advantage to the higher industrial qualities of men whose own standard of life is high.

The duties that society must discharge in its relation to the general conditions of progressive activity, and to its members who are undeveloped or degenerate, fall also into three groups. First, society must assume the regulation of international migration. Each nation must be made to bear the burden of pauperism, ignorance, and degeneracy caused by its own progress or wrong-doing. Society must also assume the regulation, by industrial and labor legislation, of those industries in which free competition displaces the better man by the inferior. Perhaps in time some of these industries may advantageously come directly under public management, as socialism proposes. Second, society must act on the fact that a proportion of its population must be always practically unfree, by extending compulsory education to the children of all parents who are unable or unwilling to provide in their own way a training that the commonwealth can approve. This education should be as perfectly adapted as knowledge, money, and sincerity of purpose can make it, to the work of fitting the children of the poor for life in a changing, progressive world. Third, society should enslave, not figuratively but literally, all those men and women who voluntarily betake themselves to a life of vagabondage. The time has passed when food and shelter should be given by kindly sentimentalists to the tramp, or when the public should deal with his case in any partial way. Every tramp within the borders of civilization should be placed under arrest and put at severe, enforced labor under public direction.

These are the positive obligations of individuals and of the State that seem to be disclosed by a study of social progress. But we must not forget that the same conditions impose a negative duty also, an obligation of restraint. For all reform, all philanthropic work, is itself a phase of social progress, and like all others, has a cost in effort and suffering. Therefore, if philanthropic reform is hurried, or pursued by too radical methods, it may convert the absolute increase of evil, which progress costs, into a relative increase, and so wholly defeat itself. Those distinguished Italian students of criminal anthropology, Lombroso and Laschi, have lately pointed out that political crime (the crime, that is, of those who unsuccessfully resist governmental authority) consists essentially in the attempt to accomplish in crude and violent ways desirable changes or reforms for which society is not yet ready. Devotion to the cause of progress these authors propose to call by the scientific name philoneism; the dread of change is misoneism. Society is on the whole misoneistic; therefore we can mend its ways but slowly. For, whatever happens, we must keep in touch with our fellow-men, remembering always the fine, true words of Marcus Aurelius : " The intelligence of the universe is social.   Accordingly it has made the inferior things for the sake of the superior, and it has fitted the superior to one another. Thou seest how it has subordinated, co-ordinated, and assigned to everything its proper portion, and has brought together into concord with one another the things which are the best."

ELECTROTYPED BY J. S. CUSHING & CO., BOSTON, U.S.A.

VII.

THE PRINCIPLES AND CHIEF DANGERS OF THE ADMINISTRATION OF CHARITY.

BY BERNARD BOSANQUET, M.A., LL.D., LONDON, ENGLAND.

No one will suppose that I intend to pass an opinion on institutions or methods of administration in the United States. I hope, before I leave this country, to see something of what is being done in Boston and New York at least. But to-day I propose to illustrate the principles of charity organization purely by London experience. It is for my hearers to judge how far anything that I say has an application that can interest them.

The principle of our work, as I understand it, is the faith in character, — the faith, if we like, in the ideal. Only it must be faith in that ideal which is the essence and controlling force of the real; not in fancies and sentiments which are simply a failure to cope with reality.

Let us plunge into our subject by asking what our title means. " Charity," it will be said, is alms-giving; "organization of charity," then, must mean "arrangements for the distribution of alms."

This is just what we do *not* mean. "Charity" for us means "neighborly service"; "organization of charity," therefore, means "concerted action in neighborly service."

The organization of charity, thus understood, involves two essential factors:

First, there must be a high and definite conception of human welfare, in so far as it can be affected by men's attempts to help their less fortunate fellows.

Secondly, there must be concerted action or division of labor in the light of this idea, and with a view to realizing it, between all persons and agencies that are attempting to do neighborly service.

In other words, it is the general principle of "organization" always to work on a plan, and that a plan based upon respect for character. The great danger is in not having any plan, and therefore interfering with other people's lives, — a most grave responsibility, — without a distinct conception of any good to be done them on the whole. Nothing undermines character so much as these chance interferences. I may illustrate this principle by the external phenomenon, observed more than twenty years ago when the London Charity Organisation Society was founded, that enough and probably far too much money was being spent in relief, apparently with the result of increasing degradation to the poor. The idea of the founders was, so far as money was concerned at all, to avoid raising more, but to try if the existing expenditure could not be made to do good instead of harm.

Now, I will try to give a picture of what we mean by "organization"; and I will begin with the work of a "District Committee." There are thirty-nine District Committees in London, one or more for each Poor Law Union; the Society consists of the federation of these committees, with a central office at 15 Buckingham Street, of which I will speak later.

Organization presupposes elements to be organized. What are the elements which we find in an average London district, with a fair mixture of rich and poor?

In the district which I have in my eye there is a population of 90,000. Judging by Mr. Charles Booth's figures, there would be in this population some 3000 "very" poor (say 700 families) and some 18,000 "poor" (4000 families). Within these (4 to 5000 families, but not including a very large proportion of them at a time) is the field of operations of charity. The comfortable working-class, numbering some 50,000, would only come in its way very occasionally and with respect to its doubtful members, or by unusual misfortune. Operating upon this "poor" popula-

tion, in all sorts of ways, there are such agencies
as these : Four old-established benevolent societies,
enjoying the confidence of the resident tradesmen,
whose charity is largely done through these societies ; six parishes of the Established Church, all
of which do relief work by different methods and
to different amounts, and some of which have
small charitable endowments ; three or four Non-
conformist organizations, attending in some degree
at least to their own poor ; and two powerful
Roman Catholic churches with the charities be-
longing to them, and with a branch of the Society
of St. Vincent de Paul.   There are three hospitals
in the district, and three more very large ones
within easy reach of it.   There is a free dispensary
(charitable), a newly-established provident dispensary, and a settlement of the district nurses who
go out to nurse the poor gratuitously in their
own homes.   Of course, there are immense numbers of charitable ladies and others who give alms
privately, and, in addition to all the rest, there
is the tremendous machinery of the Poor Law,
with its workhouse and well-equipped hospital
("infirmary") in the centre of the district, and
its schools in the country to which destitute children can be sent, and with its out-door relief,
medical relief, and dispensary — all under the
authority of a Board of Guardians, elected by
the inhabitants for this purpose.   Then there is
the system of publicly inspected primary schools

(whether "board schools" or "church schools") through which much charitable work is done, both bad and good; and there are also the very numerous charities of all sorts and kinds, which, without being especially local, are accessible to the poor of this district as to all the poor of the metropolis.

If such are the elements to be organized, what is the danger in the absence of organization? How does mischief arise from these all going their own way, regardless of each other?

We may describe the mischief done in three ways, — as doles, as overlapping, and as the downgrade to pauperism.

Doles. — Though the total expenditure on relief in such a district must be quite enormous, yet each person or agency, looking at the mass of poverty, and ignoring all other workers, feels hopelessly poor, — too poor to act on a plan. An old woman, getting past work, who is, in Charity Organization Society slang, "a pension case or nothing," has been receiving an occasional food ticket or a shilling from some agency, perhaps a church. "What good did you think you were doing by that?" you ask them. "Ah, well, we should have liked to do more; but we are so poor, and there are so many!" So no attempt is made to take hold of, and set on its feet, say, a single family. Want of faith and want of knowledge make a purpose impossible, and the aimless scattering of tickets and shillings continues. Truly, as an old woman who had thus been " helped" remarked to a friend of mine, " You know, sir, that doesn't go into deep things ! " No, indeed ! All that this practice effects is to create a gambling spirit that watches for windfalls, to encourage the desire to look poor, — for planless charity is not attracted where help is most effective, but where sentiment is most immediately touched, — and to undercut wages. The dole which enables the recipient to underbid a competitor for work makes up the difference to the recipient, but not to the competitor. The tendency in this respect is to sink wages below starvation-point by the average amount of the charitable dole.

This is bad enough ; but when you get several agencies bidding for the same poor person, the result becomes positively horrible, — it forces the poor into fraud. This is *overlapping*, — when the same person is helped, ignorantly, by several different agencies ; sometimes, alas ! by several different religious denominations. It is all very well not to let your right hand know what your left hand does ; but if your right is Presbyterian and your left Roman Catholic, and both are helping the same person, it becomes advisable that they should interchange information.

Doles and overlapping, together with the careless administration of public or semi-public relief, form the *down-grade to pauperism.* Money is to be had by luck, medical relief is to be had from charity or the Poor Law, out-door relief from the public funds may be got if you are fortunate in your application, and so people become accustomed to "chance it"; not to manage well what they have, not to make provision for so certain a case as ordinary illness, let alone a time of slack work or old age. They form the habit of going to public or semi-public offices to get benefits which they might have provided for themselves. They are not to blame. We confuse them; nothing is so pathetic as the way in which they accept what is as a guide to what should be. But it is they who have to suffer. When thrift has not been practised, and independence of character has been impaired, the end is the workhouse. We can tempt them not to provide for themselves, but we cannot and do not adequately provide for them, except in the "Union."[1] The great provident institutions which are the creation of the British working-class, and are quite unmatched in the world as proofs of character and administrative ability among the wage-earners, have no chance where unorganized charity prevails.

In such a chaos, what is the duty of a Charity Organization Committee? It is commonly spoken of as twofold, but the first branch of it really includes the second. " Organization " includes all that a District Committee should do in the way of " Relief."

---

[1] A current term for the workhouse, owing to the fact that several parishes are generally united for Poor-Law purposes.

The first and fundamental duty of the committee, then, is to "organize the district." What does this mean? Simply to bring all these people, all these agencies and institutions, into a scheme of concerted action, or division of labor, in order to work upon a plan with a view to raising the whole life of the poor. To act on a plan in every individual case, and to inform one's self what other agencies are doing and co-operate with them, are really two sides of the same procedure. For each of the institutions is fit for something; there is some want that it more especially can supply, although, in the absence of organization, it is probably (like the hospital out-departments to-day) straining to do something else, and doing it ill or harmfully. By knowing what others can do, the despair which prevented efficient work is dispelled. We try not to scatter our help over the widest possible surface, but to play our part thoroughly, and if we can only help one family, to see it through and make it self-supporting. Then something at least is done; but otherwise far worse than nothing is done. Thus, while persuading all whom it can reach of the ethical necessity for thorough work, the committee has to forward the problem in its other aspect, by charting the district, so to speak, and ascertaining *how* all might and should co-operate, and bringing them all together to determine upon co-operation. Endowed charities may be used for pensions, the benevolent societies may divide the district, and make the relief more adequate, and exchange information with other charities. "Poor-Law cases" ("unhelpable") that apply for charity may be sent to the Poor Law; "helpable" cases that apply to the Poor Law may be referred to charity. The leaders of the working class in the district should be made friends with; good provident societies made known, their juvenile branches favored, the schoolteachers consulted and interested in the thrift propaganda and in all work affecting children; the clergy should be begged — entreated — to co-operate, to give information, to let their district visitors be trained, to avoid wholesale and injurious methods of relief. The careless use of the hospitals should be checked; provident medical institutions established; sanitary law insisted on, and intelligent Poor-Law administration in every way forwarded.

That is what "organizing a district" means. The long and short of it is the transformation of a charitable chaos into an orderly and friendly neighborhood, in which rich and poor consult together and unite their resources with a clear concerted idea, not only for the relief of individual cases, but more especially for the control of general influences. When this is done, if there still are gaps in the array of institutions, they may be filled up. But, usually, there are plenty of workers and plenty of institutions, only, because the workers are untrained, and both workers and institutions are unorganized, little has been done that is beneficial, and everything that is injurious.

The task of administering relief is a secondary part of the duty of a committee, but, as things are, has to be largely undertaken. "Administering" relief must be distinguished from "providing" it, of which I will speak below. It is plain that as the committee becomes fused with the neighborhood, the relief work of the committee passes, as it ought, into the relief work of *the neighborhood in consultation.*

However this may be, all who work for or with the committee, or who advise their neighbors in relief work, should follow certain plain principles. Help should be given exactly as we give it to a friend or relation in a scrape or in misfortune. I do not think that unction and ostentatious "sympathy" are of much use, though in some trying cases the loving care of a good man or woman may make all the difference. As a rule, I should aim at a friendly business-like tone, the tone of a sympathetic lawyer or doctor. I should give no moral intention to the inquiries, but presuppose the duty of helping, if effectively possible, and simply urge that we must have the case all clear before us, if we are to find out what can be done. I do not believe that inquiries thus conducted are painful to respectable people, beyond the pain which is necessarily involved in applying for help to strangers. If the matter is put sensibly before them, they soon understand, I believe, why it is necessary to know all the family circumstances, and they appreciate the possibility that further knowledge may disclose means of help which at first did not suggest themselves. I give an instance which illustrates the nature of thorough help based on thorough knowledge.

A boy, who appeared ill-nourished, was being given half-penny dinners at school. This was the broadcast help that we condemn — too much, because too little. Inquiry showed that the family were most respectable people, but the father, a copper-worker, was unable to work through chest-disease. The wife and one boy were earning something. More than twenty pounds was raised by the Charity Organization Society for this case, with the final result of setting up the family in a different line of work, and saving it from pauperism.

It cost money, thought, and trouble, but a family was saved from pauperism. Dinners to the boy would have been useless while the family was sinking lower and lower.[1]

In case, however, of very persistent ill-luck there is almost always a screw loose in character, and for this reason again it is absolutely necessary to know the history of a case before trying to

[1] Charity Organization Society's Report of Special Committee on feeding School-children, 1891.

help. One great chance is to catch people suffering from their first folly, and then they can sometimes be set straight. Want of work through illness breaks down many a family. Illness, which would be transient, is aggravated by want of food, and seeds of delicacy are sown in wife and children at the same time. Now, every English workman, earning decent wages, can secure himself a good allowance for a long period in case of being out of work through illness, by joining one of the great Friendly Societies. The highest payment is about two pounds a year (Hearts of Oak), and secures eighteen shillings a week for six months, and a smaller allowance beyond that time. As a rule, one would not help a man in mere illness who had not done this much for himself, unless, of course, he had saved in some equivalent way. But catch him before the mischief is done, get him to join a good club *and stay in*, and you may have done well to save him from the last results of his improvidence. Refusal, with explanation, is no less important than help. People soon learn why you do and do not help. And it educates them. A charitable agency may be very fairly judged by the character of the cases that come to it. They learn that dirt and slovenliness are no claim to help; that energy and resource are qualities which the helper or helpers will gladly meet half-way; that no agency can supply the needs that spring from lack of fore-thought, industry, and management.

Relief, I said, is a form of organization. To insure this, we prefer to raise money on the case, and we are condemned, by those who know, if we employ our general funds for relief purposes.[1] Raising the money required specially on each case, though very troublesome, has immense advantages. *It enforces family ties, and neighborly or other duties,* instead of relaxing them. " Who is bound to help in this case? " is the first question, and members of the family, who may be living at a distance, are often glad to be asked, and to know that by com-bination of their resources — one giving money, another taking a child, and so on — their relatives are being effectively helped, with no contribution from strangers except advice and arrangement. Again, it *tests work ;* on every case, instead of a secretary saying, " we will do this,"·and drawing money out of the bank to do it, you have to pro-pound a plan of treatment which will secure the approval and adhesion of those who are to help, whether rich or poor. A large general fund at the bank is very dangerous. It makes you inde-pendent, and disinclined to press for money and personal help from existing agencies and persons

[1] To Americans, familiar with the Boston Associated Chari-ties and the New York Charity Organization Society, this doctrine will seem too elementary to need explaining. But I let the passage stand ; this volume may find its way to England.

bound to assist. Though we must, for the present, *administer* relief, we certainly ought not to *provide* it.

The question of visiting is not an easy one. Visitors to the same family should not be multiplied, and I think there should be, as a rule, some natural and definite reason for calling, — *e.g.*, "provident" visiting to collect sums for provident purposes. The existing visitors — clergy or district visitors — should always be utilized, if possible, when work is to be done in their districts. On the other hand, in order that this should be done, they must submit to training. The reports of an untrained lady-visitor and her advice are often abjectly useless, and to act on them would encourage fraud and all the mischiefs of charity.

As a transition from the work of District Committees to that of the central office, I may mention how convalescent aid is facilitated by the society, — a simple but efficient piece of organization. Great numbers of Convalescent Homes exist, for poor people recovering from illness. They differ in climate, in management, in the kind of cases that they will receive. If a clergyman, or other charitable individual, wants to send a poor person to a Convalescent Home, he has first to find out what home will suit the case; then, probably, to go about asking for a subscriber's letter, and then he may find that the home he has chosen has no vacancy for weeks, while another, equally suitable, could have admitted the patient at once. Through a Charity Organization Committee things are differently managed. At the central office in Buckingham Street there is a special secretary with a sub-committee containing medical men, and this secretary, among other duties, has to be in communication with all reliable Convalescent Homes accessible from London, and to secure beforehand in each of them the number of beds which experience teaches him will be needed by the society. When a convalescent case is approved by a committee, the medical certificate, and an explanatory letter, go up to the " central "; the secretary looks down his book for a suitable home at which he has a vacancy, and the admission order is sent back in a day or two at most. When, as often happens, a church pays the weekly charge at the home, or the applicant and other persons together defray it, this is a perfect piece of " organization." An immense benefit has been provided for the applicant in the promptest way, and the society has not contributed a penny except in office rents and secretaries' salaries.

The central office does no relief work. It partly supervises and supplements, as in the above instance, the work of the District Committees, and partly acts as a bureau of statistical and other information, and as a centre of propaganda and inquiry for the general public. Technically, it **is**

the "Council" office, the Council being composed
of representatives from all the committees; and
various standing committees appointed directly or
indirectly by Council meet there week by week
to control the policy and consider the work of
the society.   The District Committees in poorer
parts of London are subsidized by the Council,
and in some cases have the use of a high-class paid
secretary, who is an officer of the Council, paid
by it, and transferable from place to place at
its pleasure.   All this, of course, involves much
central supervision.

The more public work of the Council office is
at times condemned as *doctrinaire.* I often wonder
whether its critics know by what a mass of experience it is supported. Eight hundred or nine
hundred volunteer workers, besides a dozen or
more highly skilled and devoted official secretaries
on District Committees, with the forty or fifty
"agents," — men more of the type of clerks than
of secretaries, but able and experienced in the life
of their localities, — all of them are week by week
in the districts gathering the material which pours
into the central office in the shape of reports, appeals for advice, notifications of new difficulties
or new institutions, answers to circular questions
on matters of the day, and notes on prevalent helps
or hindrances in raising the life of the poor. No
investigation, I should fancy, has ever been ini-
tiated, and no policy ever adopted, at the Council

office, which has not been pressed upon it again
and again by the experience of the district workers.
Elaborate reports, with evidence, by eight or nine
special committees, appointed by the society, have
in each case carried some important social topic
into a clearer and more practical stage, from the
Report of 1875 on the Housing of the Poor, which
had much to do with the passing of Sir R. Cross's
Artisans' Dwellings Act, to the Reports on Homeless Cases, School Feeding, Insurance and Saving,
the Treatment of the Feeble-Minded and the
Organization of Medical Charities, directed to
burning questions of the most urgent importance
in 1890–92.

Another branch of work, which by itself might
occupy a less energetic organization, is the "Inquiry Work," with the resulting "cautionary
card." Week by week at the Administrative Committee, on the standing agendum "Inquiry Work,"
·the reports of the special secretary and officers —
submitted in every case to a volunteer referee —
upon institutions and individuals about which and
whom information has been asked by intending
subscribers, are carefully scanned in respect of
their thoroughness and impartiality. Not only
are rogues and frauds detected, their public support cut off, and libel actions against that "public
defendant," our secretary, successfully encountered,
but the friendly criticism which subscribers to
bona fide Societies elicit is often of service in bring-

ing about changes for the better in financial and other administration. The "cautionary card" is a list issued yearly to our subscribers of persons and institutions before assisting which it is well to communicate with the Charity Organization Society. Its utility is universally recognized.

As always, the closest grasp of facts gives the highest faith. The workers all know the power of character, and that no conditions will raise the poor, if character is sacrificed, while hard conditions can be transformed with extraordinary rapidity by ceasing to demoralize the wage-earners. In well-known examples this has been done. By abolishing out-relief in one country district of fifteen thousand souls, pauperism was reduced from about one-twelfth to about one-hundredth of the population. This is what all workers know to be natural; it is not necessity, but our folly that degrades the poor. But so low is the faith in character of those who merely write and talk and count, that no evasion is too strange for them, rather than the belief of the simplest and most natural facts. "The poor," they first said, "are driven into the workhouse by the refusal of out-relief." The figures were produced, and it was plain they were not there, for the numbers had fallen. "They were driven out into neighboring Unions." Figures were obtained, and the neighboring Unions appeared to have benefited rather than suffered. "They were living on in great poverty and misery."

Clergy and residents were consulted, and it was seen that they were doing nothing of the kind. They had turned from paupers into self-supporting citizens, as any one would expect.[1]

All these evasions of fact, and the half-hearted ideals of those who look away from reality, demand heroic measures. Proposals for these latter — such as weekly pensions for all old people over sixty-five, to be paid by the State — all rest on the persuasion that the life of the wage-earning classes cannot be organized on a business footing (taking the whole life from infancy to death as the unit to be provided for), but must in some way be supplemented from without. I do not myself believe such supplementation to be possible, in the sense of causing each man at his death to have had a larger share of wealth than a wage-system pure and simple, with proper unions and thrift-organizations, would have given him. This is for economists to decide. To me it seems to be simply cutting out some elements from the standard of life, by which, more than by anything else, we now, I suppose, consider the wage-level to be determined.

But at any rate the experiment is horribly hazardous, and wholly unnecessary. One can see

[1] The whole story may be seen in Mr. Loch's pamphlet, " Old Age Pensions and Pauperism," in reply to Mr. Chamberlain, and subsequent letters. See, also, Mr. Loch's paper in " Proceedings of Poor-Law Conference for South Wales, May, 1892." All these publications can be obtained from the London Charity Organization Society, 15 Buckingham Street, Adelphi.

the barometer of pauperism and demoralization fluctuating week by week in different divisions of the same district according to the administration. Nothing is plainer than that to an extent at present quite indefinite you can make or unmake paupers — not merely technical paupers, but poor and suffering people — at pleasure. The success of labor organization is dependent on a wise policy in this respect. When this shall have been tried to the full and shall have failed, it will be time to adopt a policy of State-supplementation, which will in all probability stereotype such evils of the wage-system as it may find existing.

I do not say that all drastic legislative reforms are bad. The present more advanced state of the dwellings question is due, as I have said, in a large measure to the initiative of the Charity Organization Society; and while futile schemes are being advocated, there are many — too many — needful reforms, well known by all experts to be desirable, which get left. I do say that legislation is all bad if and so far as it makes us forget that society is a structure of wills, and that if we do not look to the soundness of individual character — if we allow it to be perplexed and demoralized by a system of half-earnings, half-pauperism — the whole fabric must fall to pieces.